Cities, Heritage and Transformation

Series Editor
Fatemeh Farnaz Arefian, Bartlett Development Planning Unit, Silk Cities, University College London, London, UK

This book series addresses contextual and global urban challenges and opportunities that cities in historic regions face within the process of urban transformation, linked with their historic past. It publishes peer reviewed books on the relationships between the built environment, urban transformation and cultural heritage, whether to be tangible or intangible, overarched by the notion of resilience and sustainable development. Special attention is given on real-life under-explored topics. Challenging existing assumptions and disciplinary divides, the series takes an interdisciplinary position and brings together innovative researches from different areas within Geography, Social Sciences and Humanities.

The aim is to create a knowledge hub for academics and practitioners, researchers and research organisations, as well as managers and policy makers worldwide, presenting advances and case studies, which connect academia to practice.

The series benefits from the existing and growing Silk Cities' network, as well as ongoing collaborative activities Silk Cities undertake as part of its intellectual leadership on the subject matter.

The series is open for empirical, theoretical, and methodological high-quality contributions, which advance the global understanding on the subject matter. The areas covered in the series include but are not limited to the following subjects:

- Cities and intangible cultural heritage
- Community participation in managing urban heritage
- Urban history
- Urban heritage
- Cultural memory, society, and the built environment
- Development management in historic contexts
- Disaster management in historic cities
- Disaster risk reduction and resilience of historic cities and societies
- Disaster recovery and reconstruction
- Environment and historic cities
- Governing historic cities
- Geotourism and geoheritage
- Historic contexts and complex urban systems
- Post-crisis reconstruction and recovery
- Smart historic cities
- Sustainable heritage tourism
- Urban Silk Roads
- Urban economy in historic cities
- Sustainable urban heritage
- Urban conservation
- Urban design and public spaces in historic context
- Urban planning of historic cities
- Urban morphology
- Urban transformation of historic cities
- Urban connectivity and Silk Roads
- Historic cities, urban policies, and territorial planning

Hind Al-Shoubaki

War Victims and the Right to a City

From Damascus to Zaatari

Hind Al-Shoubaki
D'Annunzio University of Chieti-Pescara
Pescara, Italy

ISSN 2731-5363 ISSN 2731-5371 (electronic)
Cities, Heritage and Transformation
ISBN 978-3-031-04600-1 ISBN 978-3-031-04601-8 (eBook)
https://doi.org/10.1007/978-3-031-04601-8

© The Editor(s) (if applicable) and The Author(s), under exclusive license to Springer Nature Switzerland AG 2022
This work is subject to copyright. All rights are solely and exclusively licensed by the Publisher, whether the whole or part of the material is concerned, specifically the rights of translation, reprinting, reuse of illustrations, recitation, broadcasting, reproduction on microfilms or in any other physical way, and transmission or information storage and retrieval, electronic adaptation, computer software, or by similar or dissimilar methodology now known or hereafter developed.
The use of general descriptive names, registered names, trademarks, service marks, etc. in this publication does not imply, even in the absence of a specific statement, that such names are exempt from the relevant protective laws and regulations and therefore free for general use.
The publisher, the authors, and the editors are safe to assume that the advice and information in this book are believed to be true and accurate at the date of publication. Neither the publisher nor the authors or the editors give a warranty, expressed or implied, with respect to the material contained herein or for any errors or omissions that may have been made. The publisher remains neutral with regard to jurisdictional claims in published maps and institutional affiliations.

This Springer imprint is published by the registered company Springer Nature Switzerland AG
The registered company address is: Gewerbestrasse 11, 6330 Cham, Switzerland

Foreword

Can dwellers in refugee camps be considered residents of the place that hosts them? Moreover, can a refugee camp aspire to become a temporary city?

The work of Hind Al-Shoubaki tries to answer to these and other stimulating questions, analyzing two case studies, that of the Zaatari refugee camp in Jordan and that of the returnees to the city of Damascus in Syria. Using these examples, the author outlines the concept of a temporary city based on the principle of war victims' right to the city.

The book offers an in-depth look at the phenomenon of post-conflict temporary settlements, with specific attention to the two cases mentioned above. It proposes an integrated approach to the planning of "temporary cities," defined by the author of "Urban Emergency Integrated Planning."

The research methodology is based on the study of scientific literature and government documents; the reading of data on the conflict; an empirical and comparative investigation; and a series of interviews with refugees and other privileged interlocutors, such as experts from the UNHCR and actors of the reconstruction in Syria. The results propose an urban policy of building temporary cities capable of coping with sudden population influxes in cases of displacement and post-war reconstruction. This hypothesis is aimed at developing a new hierarchical urban planning system in agreement with territorial government bodies.

A constant tension between permanence and temporariness runs through the work, demonstrating the necessity of a comprehensive approach to managing refugees' reception, which must be open to the integration of multiple aspects. That is made necessary by a relational and moving reality, in which the form of settlements effectively binds to the process and the single parts become understandable only within a wider context, based on a system of dynamic relationship.

The work also shows how temporary cities not only are transforming into permanent structures but often produce profound impacts on the cities in which they arise, helping to shape their images and identities. Refugee camps are designed to respond to a highly pressing demand: providing asylum to large numbers of refugees in the shortest possible time. For this reason, it is understandable that quantitative aspects prevail over qualitative ones.

However, experiences such as that of Zaatari refugees show that emergency settlements often last much longer than expected and that temporary residents' needs become increasingly complex. After basic necessities have been satisfied, refugees seek to rebuild a community and give meaning and identity to the environments in which they live. With their schematic and repetitive nature, the settlement principles underlying refugee camps' spatial layouts offer few opportunities to meet these aspirations.

According to Hind Al-Shoubaki, it is necessary to renew the settlement principles and to introduce into the design criteria aimed at building places that have possibly meaning for future communities. Projects should therefore include spaces for social relations, the presence of greenery and other services, thus meeting the needs of guests as inhabitants—not only refugees waiting for an actual city. Planning can have great impact, offering opportunities to build social bonds and facilitating space-appropriation and self-construction processes.

In this regard, the author emphasizes the role of public spaces, considered as social glue for refugees who are searching for opportunities for exchange and human relations. From this perspective, the idea of the temporary city calls into question the emergency settlement project's role. It also calls into question the legislative system, designed to regulate peacetime construction process and, thus, unsuitable for managing wartime reconstruction. The creation of public spaces, such as marketplaces, squares, gardens, and children's playgrounds, can bring about essential improvements in residents' quality of life and reduce the alienation that comes from being an outsider in a monotonous space with no reference points. Hind Al-Shoubaki argues that these goals are achievable through an integrated planning approach that avoids the current separateness of the involved disciplines and renews the apparatus of often-repetitive and considerably dated techniques. The hope is that the criteria of the New Urban Agenda, which envisage more inclusive, resilient, and sustainable settlements, will be applied in the planning of temporary cities as well.

Pescara, Italy   Prof. Massimo Angrilli

Preface

The idea behind this book was initiated when I moved to Italy to get my Ph.D. in spatial planning. I decided to conduct my research coming from a different reality where cities confront complex challenges as a result of wars and conflicts. Consequently, during my Ph.D. program, my research focused on a critical issue of urban transformations: refugee camps or, as I addressed the phenomenon, "temporary cities." After discussing my dissertation, I had the definite purpose of promulgating my perspective about this phenomenon in post-war cities, and I wanted to let my voice be internationally heard. Fortunately, after a couple of great conversations with Prof. Andrew James Hopkins, I was able to meet with the genius Prof. Farnaz Arefian, who was gracious enough to review my book proposal.

As you will see, this book discusses war victims' right to a city. In other words, the need for refugees and citizens returning to their homelands after wars to have a real, permanent, functional city. It presents a framework that links urbicide, emergency management, and integrated urban planning to discuss refugees' immediate need for a city, using as evidence the issue of post-conflict displacement resulting from the Syrian civil war. Consequently, it describes the need for a new urban agenda to provide fully functional cities for two types of war victims: refugees in host countries and those returning to their homelands. This book discusses this urgent need within two critical cases: the Syrian refugees in the Zaatari refugee camp and the repatriate population in Damascus. It assesses their current conditions, filling the gaps in urban politics that deal with post-conflict reconstructions. The novelty of this study is in creating this cross-case synthesis that helps to draw the rights of war victims in a real city, not a shelter or a camp. Beyond that, this study contributes to the literature by creating a conceptual framework for post-conflict reconstruction in the case of the Syrian civil war. In summary, this book provides a novel, comprehensive conceptual framework for post-conflict reconstruction, which represents a step toward understanding how to deal with the urgent need for housing with more long-term outcomes that will help in advancing a new urban agenda for internal and external developers in the reconstruction field.

This book has been an enormous undertaking and could not have been accomplished without the help and support of many people to whom I owe so much gratitude, but I will try to keep it brief. As I mentioned previously, I am grateful to Prof. Farnaz Arefian for giving me the opportunity to present my book idea and for her guidance, creative control, and insightful thoughts. I look forward to our next opportunity to collaborate. I would also like to express my sincere gratitude to my Ph.D. mentor, Prof. Zazzara and my postdoc mentor Prof. Angrilli, for their profound belief in my work and my abilities. I would also like to extend my sincere thanks to all the people who have become part of this study: the refugees in the Zaatari refugee camp and the engineers, experts, professors, and policymakers from Damascus for their collaboration, invaluable contributions, suggestions, and experience.

Finally, the writing of this book could not have been achieved without the great support of some very special people, and it is dedicated to them. One is my source of inspiration, my husband Ehab, who helped me tackle every difficulty. Thank you for your love, affection, and unwavering support. Special thanks to my family in Amman and Rome for their encouragement along the way.

Lugano, Switzerland   Hind Al-Shoubaki

Contents

1 **Introduction: The Temporary City** 1
  1.1 The Temporary City Hypothesis 5
  1.2 The Relationship Between the Camp and Neighborhood 13
  1.3 Jordan and Zaatari Camp 18
  1.4 Syria and Damascus City 26
  1.5 How Cities Absorb and Deal with the Sudden Population
      Influx and the Need for Urban Housing? 27
      1.5.1 The C.A.S.E Project in L'Aquila—The Abruzzo
             Region—Italy 27
      1.5.2 An Adequate Urban Housing for Refugees
             in the Thessaloniki-Greece 30
      1.5.3 The Refugee Camps as an Alternative—Jordan 33
  1.6 The Structure of the Book 37
  1.7 Conclusion 38
  References 39

2 **The Urbicide** 43
  2.1 The Concept of Urbicide 43
  2.2 Direct Urbicide in Syrian Cities 45
  2.3 Indirect Urbicide, "Conflict-Induced Displacement
      and the Right to the City" 48
  2.4 Post-conflict Urban Reconstruction and Redefining a Place
      to Live In 51
  2.5 Urban Emergency Management and Developing an Integrated
      Approach to Planning 54
      2.5.1 The Methodology Process of an Integrated Planning 56
  2.6 Conclusion 58
  References 59

3 **Spaces in Emergency** 63
  3.1 Direct Urbicide: Damascus City in Syria 63
      3.1.1 The Urban Development of Damascus 64

		3.1.2	From a Strong Classical Geometric Pattern to a Compact Organic Urban Form: Greco-Roman Damascus and Islamic Damascus Urban Matrix	64
		3.1.3	Reviving the Geometric Master Plan Layout: The Ottoman Damascus and Damascus Under the French Mandate	67
		3.1.4	Informal Settlements in Damascus	73
	3.2	Damascus Urban Scenario in Wartime		76
	3.3	The Syrian Approach in Construction: An Eye Over the Organization Laws in Syria		80
		3.3.1	The Law 10	82
		3.3.2	The Law No. 33	83
		3.3.3	Law 9	84
	3.4	Assessing the Damage, Especially in the Housing Sector in an Aim to Determine the Real Need for City		85
	3.5	The Indirect Urbicide: Zaatari Refugee Camp in Jordan		85
		3.5.1	Jordan Urban Scenario: High Level of Urbanization with Poor Planning Strategies	86
		3.5.2	Zaatari Refugee Camp	88
		3.5.3	The Population Growth in Zaatari Refugee Camp	88
		3.5.4	The Zaatari Camp, Urban Housing, and Spatial Planning: The Abrupt Space for Emergency	90
	3.6	Conclusion		93
	References			93
4	**Urban Emergency Integrated Planning UEIP**			**97**
	4.1	The Spatial Sphere		98
	4.2	Diagnostic Sphere		100
	4.3	Construction Laws and the Technical Standards Sphere		104
	4.4	UEIP: Urban Emergency Integrated Planning		108
	4.5	Conclusion		112
	References			112
5	**Concluding Discussions**			**115**
	5.1	UEIP and FUTURE Directions		115
	5.2	Conclusion		120
	References			121
Index				**123**

Abbreviations

FEMA	Federal Emergency Management Agency
IDP	Internally Displaced Person
OCHA	The Office for the Coordination of Humanitarian Affairs
PCR	Post-Conflict Reconstruction
REACH	Informing More Effective Humanitarian Action
SWP	The German Institute for International and Security Affairs
UEIP	Urban Emergency Integrated Planning
UN	United Nation
UNDP	The UN Development Program
UNHCR	The UN Refugee Agency
UNITAR	United Nations Institute for Training and Research
UNOSAT	UN Operational Satellite Application Program
UNRWA	The UN Relief and Works Agency for Palestine Refugees in the Near East
WHO	World Health Organization

Chapter 1
Introduction: The Temporary City

Abstract This chapter introduces the refugee camps as a unique form of human habitation that is transitionally born between the war and the city and plays a formative role in the city's urban fabric. This chapter explores the temporary city phenomenon through two main streams: Firstly, the relationship between the camp and its neighborhood—secondly, the cities' response to the sudden population influx and the need for urban housing, which have been reviewed in this chapter within three main approaches; the Italian approach, the Greek approach, and the Jordanian approach. Consequently, the first section of this chapter puts in evidence the formation and transformation of refugee camps and the reasons behind their hazardous transformation into slum-like zones lacking spatial hierarchy between the camp cluster and the city urban fabric furthermore, how the temporary shelters transform gradually into a permanent settlement forming a unique urban entity which notably impacts the whole urban identity of the zones where they appeared. Conspicuously, a primordial form of a city is born when the canvas fields begin to be replaced by more durable structures. It is not only a matter of materials but also the beginning of a historical process representing the time and sedimentation of the habitat: the history of the city. History as a continuous change is a city's most crucial dimension; it measures its greatness, culture, and absolutely its identity.

Keywords Temporary city · Refugee camp · Spatial transformation

Rapid urbanization, migration, natural incidents, conflicts or wars bring about a displaced population, which shapes a burden on housing, the infrastructures, the urban environment, and the community demographics and cohesion (Cattaneo, 2020). Recently, The Syrian civil war has generated a distinctive urban phenomenon regarding the displaced population's need for a city. In fact, the Syrian refugees' mass flow to the surrounding countries, especially Jordan, Lebanon, and Europe, produced a decline in the Syrian republic's total population and required the hosting countries to deal with this sudden population influx by accommodating them in refugee camps. In contrast, the population in Damascus, the capital, has been perilously increased. The internally displaced persons who fled from the conflicted zones to the capital are equally in real need of safe housing. To investigate this phenomenon, the Syrian conflict-induced displaced population was chosen. The rationale for this comes from the fact that the Syrian refugee crisis is considered as the most significant ongoing refugee crisis all over the world (reliefweb, 2019). More than 5.6 million Syrians are refugees, and 6.6 million are internally displaced in Syria (UNHCR, 2020a, b, c, d). In other words, the Syrian civil war has displaced half of Syria's pre-war population into neighboring countries like Jordan, Turkey, Lebanon, Iraq, and Egypt. In contrast, the other half is internally displaced (reliefweb, 2019). The characteristics of the chosen displaced population fit the research framework because the phenomenon under investigation could be analyzed for their refuge and repatriation. From one side, up to this moment, the escalated conflict and civil war in Syria generates new masses of displaced populations as recently on the ninth of October 2019, nearly 160,000 Syrians have been displaced because of the Turkish military attack (reliefweb, 2019). From the other side, Syrian's displaced populations—internally and internationally—are returning to their place of origin voluntarily or forcibly, as tracked by NPM project in the period from January to October 2017, that 766,852 had returned to Syria, about 4000 from Turkey, 4300 from Jordan, and 4500 from Lebanon (iDMC, 2017). Accordingly, this book discusses the displaced Syrian population issue via two directions: Firstly: the Syrian refugees in Jordan who were accommodated in the Zaatari refugee camp which was instituted in 2012, close to the Northern border with Syria. Secondly: the returnees to their homeland, specifically Damascus, the Syrian capital, who are in urgent need of housing in totally or partially destroyed zones.

In an effort to better understand the role of integrated spatial planning in building sustainable urban housing in post-conflict situations, the two selected cases, Zaatari refugee camp and Damascus city, have been analyzed within three main spheres: the spatial sphere, the construction laws, and the technical standards sphere, as well as the diagnostic and assessment sphere. The three spheres have been utilized as an analytical strategy to confront the two cases' complexity, attain a better comparative analysis, and identify the current spatial, organizational, and regulatory conditions of the two selected cases. This strategy has been chosen as a guidance trail to anatomize this research process's intricacy, control the parameters of the cases under investigation, and avoid being lost in the collected data and the analysis progress. Utilizing cross-case synthesis as a research tool: a qualitative analysis of the two cases, a systematic review of gray literature and peer-reviewed articles, and semi-structured interviews, which are frequently used in spatial planning research because they provide flexibility and openness to new information, questions, and issues (MacCallum et al., 2019). Interviews have been conducted with refugees—males and females—in the Zaatari refugee camp, experts in the reconstruction field in Syria, academics, and researchers in urban planning, environmental engineering, habitat engineering, and structural engineering, as documented in Table 1.1.

Alongside that, introducing an innovative conceptual framework: Urban Emergency Integrated Planning (UEIP), which emerged to handle the post-conflict displacement resulting from the Syrian civil war through the temporary city hypothesis, which entails the necessary urban politics to provide permanent, fully functional cities for two types of war victims: refugees in host countries, and returnees to their homelands and to stretch the boundaries of urban planning theories to cover planning in emergencies, to attain better long-term resettlement after wars through the

Table 1.1 Interviews conducted in the Zaatari refugee camp and Damascus

Case	Occupation	Date of interview	Language of interview/translation	City of origin	City of residence
Damascus city	A full Professor in Environmental Engineering at the University of Damascus & The head of the department of Environmental Development at the High Institute of Regional Planning	April-27-2020	English	Damascus-Syria	Damascus-Syria
Damascus city	Assistant Professor in the Department of Planning and Environment at the Faculty of Architecture of the University of Damascus. and The Deputy Dean of the Higher Institute for Regional Planning, and The Head of the Logistical Regional Planning Department at the Higher Institute of Regional Planning/Damascus	May-5-2020	Arabic/translated by the researcher	Damascus -Syria	Damascus-Syria
Damascus city	Expert in Construction claims-litigation and Arbitration with Diploma in Refugee and Forced Migration Studies at the Center for Strategic Studies and A lawyer with the United Nations for The Human Rights	July-12-2020	Arabic/translated by the researcher	Dara'a -Syria	Amman-Jordan

(continued)

Table 1.1 (continued)

Case	Occupation	Date of interview	Language of interview/translation	City of origin	City of residence
Damascus city	Structural Engineer/ Ph.D. in Structural Engineering/ Cairo University	Aug-17-2020	Arabic/translated by the researcher	Damascus-Syria	Cairo-Egypt
Damascus city	Environmental and Habitat Engineer/International Committee of The Red Cross in Syria Master in Structural Engineering at the University of Damascus	Aug-21-2020	Arabic/translated by the researcher	Raqqa -Syria	Hasakah -Syria
Damascus city	Environmental and Mechanical engineer/Douma Local Council	Aug-22-2020	Arabic/translated by the researcher	Douma, Rif Dimashq -Syria	Istanbul-Turkey
Zaatari refugee camp	Refugee	April-17-2020	Arabic/translated by the researcher	Dara'a	Zaatari since 2017
Zaatari refugee camp	Refugee	April-21-2020	Arabic/translated by the researcher	Eastern Ghouta	Zaatari since 2013
Zaatari refugee camp	Refugee	April-23-2020	Arabic/translated by the researcher	Dara'a	Zaatari since 2013
Zaatari refugee camp	Refugee	April-23-2020	Arabic/translated by the researcher	Dara'a	Zaatari since 2013

Own illustration

integrated spatial planning, with an aim to shift the policies of emergency from short-term response to long-term recovery where the numbers of refugees and displaced communities are rapidly growing and changing while the urban frame is still adapting very slowly with no appropriate policies to deal with this kind of sudden population influx in cities.

In fact, this research promotes an innovative sustainable resettlement planning for conflict-stricken communities by highlighting the permanency as the new temporality; which will help emergency managers and humanitarian organizations to attain adequate and durable housing solutions and providing a sustainable humanitarian relief for refugees and persons of concern.

This research highlights the need for a new urban agenda to provide fully functional cities for two types of war victims: refugees in host countries, and returnees to their homelands. The selected population of Syrian war victims and the selected urban context are unique. There is no previous cross-case analysis for the city of Damascus and the Zaatari refugee camp in terms of the right of stricken people to a city.

This book contributes to the global literature in bringing the discussion of an urgent need to a city within such two critical cases: the Syrian refugees in the Zaatari refugee camp, and the repatriate population in Damascus. It assessed their current conditions to fill the gaps in the implemented politics literature dealing with post-conflict reconstruction (PCR). The novelty of this study is in creating this cross-case synthesis to draw the rights of war victims in an actual city, not a shelter or a camp. It offers a conceptual framework for PCR in the case of the Syrian civil war, which linked the integrated urban planning theory with urban emergency management to fill the gaps in the current reconstruction laws in Syria. This study introduced a new term to the literature of urbicide, the "indirect urbicide," used to describe the indirect violence to the cities' urban tissue in the case of refugee camps. The comprehensive conceptual framework for PCR) is a step toward understanding how to deal with the urgent need for housing with more long-term outcomes that help in advancing a new urban agenda for internal and external developers in the reconstruction field.

1.1 The Temporary City Hypothesis

Refugee camps are a unique form of human habitation; they are the transitional spaces born between "war and city," and they play a formative role in the city's urban fabric. They are the types of settlements connected to emergencies following human-made disasters such as conflicts, wars, or any kind of terrorist action or following natural incidents like earthquakes, hurricanes, and tornadoes. This type of settlement has a temporary character, in which they are not connected to the urban fabric or the historical development of the hosting countries' lands because they are hanging to the state of exception as "accidental cities" where they are seeking quick solutions. They forget that any type of construction requires a long time typically. As time passes, the refugees accept the fact that their dream of returning is not so close—it may be possible but will occur at an unknown time. Thus, families begin looking beyond shelters and perceive their new settlements as definitive houses, despite their provisional character. From this moment, the sense of city starts shaping these camps. And what begins as temporary shelter transforms gradually into permanent settlements, and this provisional settlement hits its roots in the city's urban tissue, forming a unique urban entity that impacts the urban identity of the zones where they appear.

The fact is that the world now is witnessing a significant acceleration in the numbers of uprooted people because of local, regional, national, and international armed conflicts, wars, or natural incidents like earthquakes, volcanos, hurricanes, and tornados. These events shape a new spatial phenomenon: the refugee camps which impact the urban tissue form and identity.

In point of fact, it is not a new phenomenon. Still, it has gradually taken great attention from individuals, organizations, and governments because of the negative consequences of the implemented strategies in constructing refugee camps since the main goal is to provide humanitarian relief for the refugees using very light structures and temporary materials (Ramadan, 2013).

Historically, these kinds of so-called temporary settlements were spread in ancient Rome to accommodate the inhabitants from unexpected Tiber river floods in "Campus Martius" (Hailey, 2009). In fact, the emergence of refugee camps was coupled with the Second World War and became much more notable after the Cold War (Gale, 2008). The most significant number of refugees was 60 million during the Second World War (1939–1945). The second-largest number of refugees resulted from the Syrian civil war (2011–2021) when 11.6 million people were forced to leave their homes; 6.5 million were internally displaced. The rest has fled to their neighboring countries like Jordan, Iraq, and Lebanon. The third-largest number of displaced persons was in 1948, according to the Israeli–Palestinian conflict. Around 5.1 million registered Palestinian refugees in 60 camps in the middle east (Zampano et al., 2015).

Accordingly, the world has always examined different internal conflicts and wars that increase the number of refugees. Therefore, the number of refugees' camps and provisional cities has grown more and more. In fact, by 2015, the global refugee population reached 65.3 million (UNHCR, 2015). The Syrian crisis is considered one of the most prolonged crises since the Second World War and one of the worst humanitarian catastrophes in our times (SBS, 2013). Currently, there are 27 major active conflicts that impact the increase in the number of refugee camps (Koop, 2021). The unceasing conflicts and incidents mean that people are constantly suffering from being refugees or internally displaced, and that the construction of the refugee camps is also increasing. The refugees' camps vary according to their size, shape, and life span. Some camps have been constructed to lodge around 50 people like the Sri Lankan refugees in India; other camps accommodated more than 150.000 people, such as Burundi refugees in Tanzania (Magrinà, 2006). Refugee camps also have a different life span; for example, the Palestinian refugee camps have been lasted more than 65 years. Looking at the world's largest refugee camp; the Dadaab refugee camp in Garissa County in Kenya, which was constructed between 1990 and 2011(UNHCR, 2014). The camp has been transformed into a semi-structured city, and it is divided into five sections, namely, Dagahaley, Ifo, Ifo2, Hagadera, and

1.1 The Temporary City Hypothesis

Kambioos as shown in Fig. 1.1. The camp has 19 primary schools and six secondary schools that serve 156.000 school-aged children. One referral center with 100-beds offers special and secondary services, and most refugees inside the Dadaab complex participate in different activities such as farming, fishing, and trading (UNHCR, 2014). Accordingly, refugee camps are the most adapted strategy to host the refugees and become an essential landscape feature of any humanitarian crisis since around forty percent of all refugees live in camps (UNHCR, 2013).

As Bauman (2001: 266) said "if common consent and history books establish the seventeenth century as the age of reason, the eighteenth century as the age of enlightenment and the nineteenth century as the age of revolutions, the best name to describe the twentieth century is the age of camps."

The problem is that the response to catastrophic events has been the same since the Second World War (WWII), that is to construct refugee camps under the arc of short-term solutions, focusing on emergency strategies to cope with refugee crises quickly and with low-cost. In fact, there are no quick fixes for the refuge causes. Therefore, the destiny of these zones is to be a new part of the urban fabric of the neighboring cities. The camps' residents also take roots in the land, thus giving birth to troublesome slums. It is essential to mention that the average duration of significant refugee situations has increased from nine years in 1993 to seventeen years in 2003 (UNHCR, 2004).

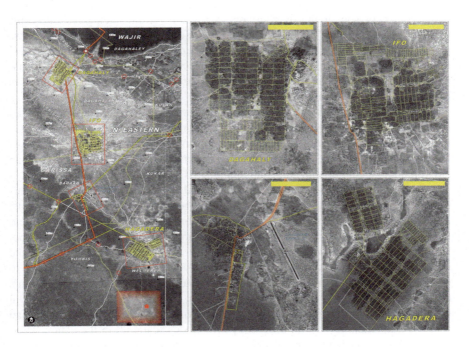

Fig. 1.1 Dadaab refugee camps overview-Garissa, N-Eastern, Kenya. Ref: UNOSAT (2009)

Refugee camps exist in a state of continuous transformation as residents shape them into semi-functional cities. With time, they grow to be part of the host countries' urban fabric or evolve into urban centers that gradually take on a permanent character and rapidly transform their urban, environmental, social, cultural, and economic features. The metamorphosis of refugee camps into decaying cities results from the continuous increase in population density and the physical modifications carried out by the refugees based on their needs. They shape arbitrary expansion over a long period. In fact, the population density inside camps evolves over time based on two main factors: the natural growth rate and the continuous arrival of refugees due to forced displacement. A good example is the Zaatari refugee camp, which has developed from a small collection of tents that hosted 30,000 Syrian refugees in 2012 into an urban settlement that housed 80,000 refugees in 2021 (UNHCR, 2021) due to the continuous arrival of Syrian refugees. Seeking safety, more than 1500 refugees crossed the border every night. In addition, the birth rate increased from 13–15 births registered in 2013 (UNHCR, 2015). Another similar scenario could be seen in one of the Palestinian refugee camps in Jordan, Al-Baqa'a camp which is an emergency camp located 20 km north of Amman was instituted with 5000 tents to lodge 26.000 refugees, Palestinian refugees, after the 1967 Arab–Israeli war. The camp is considered the largest refugee camp in Jordan, and it now accommodates around 100.000 Palestinian refugees over an area of 1.4 km^2 (UNRWA, 2017). The population density in the Al-Baqa'a camp in Jordan is remarkably high, with more than 100,000 persons living over an area of 1.4 km^2 (Ammannet, 2015). It seems to have higher density rates than Mumbai and Kolkata, where the density is less than 30,000 persons per kilometer. Camps grew up with time to meet the refugees' needs shaping an "iconic city." In the same token, camps' structures, all over history, have been modified by the refugees themselves based on their needs, as described in Fig. 1.2 in the Al-Baqa'a refugee camp.

Despite the fact that at the beginning the Palestinian refugees refused any kind of infrastructural development as they were looking for a quick return because they thought that it was gesturing their acceptance for permanent resettlement outside of Palestine. But, after more than 60 years, the camp transformed into a complex urban environment lacking organization and planning (Barqawi, 2014).

The temporary status of refugees' camps is also linked to the restriction rules that prevent further expansions from the determined area by hosting governments. The United Nations Relief and Works Agency for Palestine Refugees in the Near East "UNRWA" has decided to rearrange the Baqa'a camp into a grid-like layout with 100 m^2 plots known as "the right of use." This "right of use" allowed the refugees: Firstly: to build a (3 × 4 m) asbestos room within the plot. Secondly: to replace the tents with more durable materials such as mud, concrete, stone, iron, zinc, and asbestos (UNRWA, 2017). A few years later, refugees started their horizontal expansion over the 100 m^2 plot to build their own amenities. Previously, they had shared these amenities within different public nodes scattered in the camp. Later, refugees had implemented new architectural elements to their spaces, such as the threshold (Maqusi, 2014). By the 1980–1990s, the plots could not bear any horizontal

1.1 The Temporary City Hypothesis

Baqa'a refugee camp 1967.
Ref: UNRWA audiovisual archives, https://unrwa.photoshelter.com/galleries.

Baqa'a refugee camp 1970.
Ref: UNRWA audiovisual archives, https://unrwa.photoshelter.com/galleries.

Baqa'a refugee camp 2020.
Ref: By the author from google maps 2020

Baqa'a refugee camp 2018.
Ref: https://prc.org.uk/.

Fig. 1.2 The transformation of Al Baqa'a refugee camp from field of tents in to a decaying city. Ref: The author from UNRWA and google maps 2018

expansions; at this point, refugees tended to go vertically by implementing stairs as a new architectural element.

The same scenario reappears in the Zaatari camp as it transforms on the infrastructure level, spatial organization, and residential unit scale. The camp grows through the development of the education system, economy, livelihoods, open spaces, medical centers, and the transformation of the residential units from tents to prefabricated caravans. The new caravans are new immobile prefabricated shelters consisting of one kitchen and one wash facility supplied with wastewater and water supply. They also extended the living spaces to fulfill refugee aspirations for more space and hygiene facilities (UNHCR, 2016). In short, the transformation of the Baqa'a camp into a permanent city has been developed by the refugees themselves in different ways, either by using solid and hard materials or by vertical expansion and horizontal construction. In the case of the Zaatari camp, the refugees employed their skills using graphics and paintings to make their caravans more livable. As well, they grew plants and vegetation around their caravans. This kind of conversion indicates that refugees are conscious that the camp will be their home for a more extended period and have a longing for a more solid settlement.

The temporary mindset in designing refugee camps increases the complexity and hardship of the refugees' daily life because their personal needs will develop as a response to the natural life process. The evolution of individuals' needs within a physical space is a critical factor that leads the transformation of the camp from a sheltering settlement into a semi-structural city with hard materials. Remarkably, a primordial form of a city is born when the fields of canvas begin to be replaced by structures that are more durable. It is not only a matter of materials but also the beginning of a historical process representing the time and sedimentation of the habitat: the history of the city. History as a process of continuous change is a city's most crucial dimension; it is the measure of its greatness, culture, and absolutely its identity.

The response of spatial planners and urban politicians to emergencies usually requires speedy solutions within a short time and at minimum cost. Consequently, they employ incremental planning strategies by designing refugee camp settlements based on numbers and minimum standards, which shape the temporary character of these spaces.. Refugee camps generally developed in "Autoschediasm" mode, suddenly, unexpectedly, and at the spur of the moment to provide refugees with basic needs quickly and for a short period. In most cases, the camps settlements constructed depending on manuals and guidelines that have been developed by humanitarian organizations, such as the Handbook for Emergencies (UNHCR, 2007a, b); Refugee Camp Planning and Construction Handbook (2000); and The Sphere Handbook: Humanitarian Charter and Minimum Standards in Disaster Response (2004) (Alshoubaki & Zazzara, 2020). Many academics and designers considered refugee camps as an urban environment, which is a production of political, economic, environmental, and social life (Grbac, 2013). In 1977, Cuny discussed his vision "camp as a city" and the significant role of refugees in the spatial reconstruction of the camp based on their needs. On this, he analyzed the physical spatial zoning of the refugee camp according to firstly the camp physical elements such as shelters and sewage systems; secondly, the distribution of services to serve camp inhabitants. Similarly, Jennings (2001) mentioned that not only the form constructs the physical layout of the city, but the community's rituals, traditions, customs, and behaviors play an essential role in shaping the city structure. Conceptualizing refugee camps as cities will help to improve the quality of refugees' life as these camps built as a temporary response to an emergency. It is essential to mention that the average duration of major refugee situations has increased from nine years in 1993 to seventeen years in 2003 (Refworld, 2007b; UNHCR, 2004). So, planners and urban politicians should pay close attention to the issue of permanency of these camps as Kleinschmidt (2015) expressed what is happening in the middle east where camps built as spaces to storage people but refugees shaping and constructing their own spaces. The technical standards for the camp planning focus on the temporary character as a main feature during the first phase of the emergency. Subsequently, the temporary mindset creates serious problems and transforms those temporary structures into ramshackle cities, putting the displaced persons among the most vulnerable populations (Alshoubaki, 2018). Many guidebooks, reports, and research papers set up various visions to construct refugee camps under the arc of short-term solutions, focusing on emergency strategies to cope with refugee crises quickly with low-cost solutions. Generally, there are two types of refugee camps planning; the first one is the grid plan, which is the most preferred strategy in case of an emergency where it is quick and easy to apply. In the grid plan, the neighborhoods are being formed by the network system of roads as in the organizational structure of the Zaatari refugee camp shown in Fig. 1.3. This method increases accessibility, control, and security of the camp, but according to refugees, it reduces the sense of community, privacy, and belonging. A refugee from Dara'a who has lived in Zaatari since 2013 said that the quality of life and how the camp districts were distributed impacted their sense of belonging and thus the community spirit. He stated, "I can't easily reach my relatives who live in another district because of the distance and poor street networks". In fact, the camp layout, the residential unit size, and design affect the refugees' comfort and well-being; as confirmed by a Syrian woman, "In Zaatari, we suffer from the lack of privacy, the residential units don't offer minimum privacy to do our activities."

Fig. 1.3 Zaatari refugee camp in Jordan. Ref: UNITAR-UNOSAT 2014

Fig. 1.4 Al-Azraq refugee camp in Jordan. Ref: UNICEF, 2014

The second strategy is the cluster planning approach, which applies different sizes and shapes of roads providing public areas within private spaces to increase the sense of community by sharing activities between neighborhoods (D'Ettorre, 2016) as the implemented planning strategy of hierarchical spatial differentiation in Al-Azraq camp in Jordan. The camp which was officially opened in 2014 (UNHCR, 2021), it was organized into four villages that house the refugees and one for managing the camp see Fig. 1.4.

The humanitarian aid organizations drew general guidelines that had been developed from 1906 until now. Pawar, Epstein, and Simon (2015) mentioned that in 1906, the first document was written to manage the situation for people affected by the San Francisco earthquake where the army corps of engineers used the military-style camp to provide 5000 shelters to lodge more than 40.000 displaced person (Architecture for Humanity, 2006, p. 33). This planning still used in the current design of refugee camps. In 1971, Fred Cuny developed a refugee camp design framework according to the "Community-based" approach (Kennedy, 2008, p.81). Howard and spice (1973) discussed the use of plastic sheeting for emergency shelters, and the instructions used to develop Oxfam technical guide. Kennedy (2008, p.92) reviewed the design of khula camp in Bangladesh after the flood of 1973. Where Cuny involved the local community in designing shelters and layout of the camp. In 1982 the first full edition of the United Nation High Commissioner for Refugees "UNHCR" handbook of emergencies was issued based on Cuny vision "camp as a city" (Kennedy, 2008, p.113). By 1995 humanitarian aids started managing, designing, and planning refugee camps in terms of numbers where it released a list of minimum standards of living conditions according to cost and budget (Scavino, 2014). UNHCR (2007a, b) developed different benchmarks to plan and manage refugee camps, starting from planning methods where it proposed three different types of planning, namely, modular planning, decentralization, and the "bottom-up" approach. Considering that planning plays an important role in shaping refugees' social life, security, and protection. The framework also implied the effect of climatic conditions on local health and how vegetation, including grass, bushes, shrubs, and trees, enhances shade and decreases soil erosion and dust within the camp environment. It also recommends a minimum surface area of 45 m^2 per person, including kitchen and gardening space where a bare minimum surface area is 30 m^2, and it recommended the shelter space per person to be 3.5 m^2. The minimum distance between two shelters has to be 2 m; besides, each restroom has to serve 20 people, and each water-point serves 250 people with a maximum distance to water point is 15 m where the distance to latrine is 30 m. The distance between water-point and latrine is 100 m. Cuny (1977) investigated the importance of dealing with refugee camps as cities where they must fulfill their inhabitants' needs, providing them with housing, roads, parks, open areas, water, electricity, health centers, security units, schools, and libraries.

The international agencies such as the UN organizations involved in dealing with emergencies tend to work on "one size fits all." They often don't develop the work strategies based on the context of crisis, but they come to the emergency field carrying their package of organizational, operational, and executive policies (Earnest, 2015).

Turning a blind eye to the context is the crux of the problem, the rigidity in working with emergency and the implemented planning methods and techniques are not suitable anymore but instead worsen it. The current planning strategies in construction refugee camps create temporary cities with low qualities that impact the urban fabric identity as well as provide a provisional settlement that has no decent relationship with the neighborhood. Building resilience requires strong roots that anchor the policy to the context using a "context-specified" approach, but it needs flexible branches to adapt to unpredictable conditions. The incremental type of planning in the current design of refugee camps neglects the camp's relationship with the cities' urban fabric and the refugees' needs, desires, and aspirations. In addition, the planning does not consider the fact that architecture and services have to maintain human rights because camps need to be not only safe but also to provide the right living conditions and have appropriate relationships with the neighborhoods where they appear. As illustrated in Fig. 1.5, the spot light of the current implemented strategies in constructing the refugee camps only illuminates a small part of the refuge journey, leaving the rest of their life under the shadows.

1.2 The Relationship Between the Camp and Neighborhood

The urban scenery of the refugee camps could be comprehended based on the camp transformation and the growth of the city's spatial structure. Usually, the refugee camps constructed on the peripheries, which then become a central neighborhood

Fig. 1.5 The transformation story of refugee camps (illustration by the author, 2018)

Burj Al-Barajneh camp in Lebanon

Hittin camp in Jordan

Al-Baqa'a camp in Jordan

1.2 The Relationship Between the Camp and Neighborhood

because, over time, the city's spatial footprint expands and what was considered outskirts transform into a nucleus of the city geographically and historically. As could be seen in Fig. 1.6 where the Palestinian refugee camps in Amman are now shaping the core of the Jordanian capital due to the rapid urban growth that Amman witnessed within less than 100 years.

Consequently, this form of settlement gradually integrates with the city's urban tissue and gives a specific identity to the whole urban scenery. The question to be raised is on the relationship between the refugee camp with the grown city over its urban tissue and if the refugee camps—overtime—blend with neighborhood spatial configuration?

To answer this question, we should shed light on the clusters' formation process of settlement, whether by refugees, internally displaced, or immigrants on the edge of

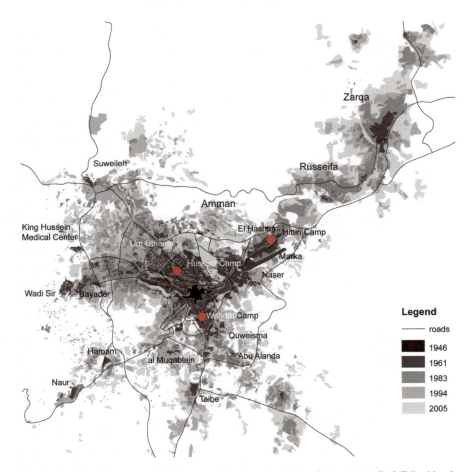

Fig. 1.6 Amman city expansion in reference to the Palestinian refugee camps. Ref: Edited by the author 2020 from Ifpo 2009

the city, where they create adjustments on the hosting city's urban environments. This configuration process could either occur at a slow pace, as in the case of immigrants or a sudden quick manner, as in the case of refugee camps. Settlement clustering impacts the cities' urban form and shapes urban segregation because of the physical separation between spaces and between people's activities (Legeby, 2010). As argued by Vaughan (1997) in her paper, the urban ghetto that "the modern malaise of segregation and isolation of minority groups is invariably blamed on the spatial polarization prevalent in cities today."

The transformation of refugee camp settlement, as mentioned before, is connected to the evolving of daily life necessities over a specific urban context and because the quotidian and the urban are inextricably intertwined as they are products and producers that occupy a social space built through them and vice versa. Consequently, understanding the refugee camp phenomenon in cities should go beyond studying it as a system or a temporary structure in the classical sense of the term but instead to analyze and synthesize the connection of its structural elements and its social, economic, political aspects with the urban setting. The analysis should focus on the set of practical-social activities and on their intertwining in a sophisticated urban and daily space that ensures, to a certain extent, the reproduction of the relationships between the camp and its neighborhood, and they are spatial relationships, social relationships, and socio-spatial relationships.

The configuration of a refugee camp occurs to meet the accumulation of quotidian needs and accommodate behaviors. Thus, a so-called camp begins taking the shape of a permanent city that represents a specific relationship with its surrounding context. It is not an ideological representation of displacement but a physical reality that exemplifies the spatial configuration of the social interaction with political mediation through a set of rules that govern the camp rehabilitation process. The refugee camp has a specificity that carries out an aspect of general discourse of city planning up to a certain level in which the city evolvement and the growing urban fabric are combined to a sudden population. It is not an issue of natural growth but a sudden mass influx of refugees absorbed by the city. The transformation story of the refugee camp in the city is narrating a continuous change of space across time over the hosting city urban fabric, turning a blinded eye to the hosting city's historical, cultural, and spatial measures. This hazardous transformation leads the cities to the point of no return and non-appeal.

The temporary city hypothesis is about a spatial organization that deals with a sudden population in case of displacement, whether internally or out of borders. It helps us to understand the transformation of refugee camps from provisional settlements into slum-like neighborhoods. The complexity of this transformation is in the lack of spatial hierarchy between the camp cluster and the urban city fabric. It is not to show structural coherence and cohesion within the camp components but to try, groping, by attempts, to place and to understand this unique urban phenomenon within a specific frame of time and space. Over time, camps metamorphose until they reach the point of no return and non-appeal. This occurs not on the scale of the camp cluster or its neighborhood but the country scale because the morphology of the refugee camp has an inferior quality of infrastructure with a very high population

1.2 The Relationship Between the Camp and Neighborhood

density. For this reason, the camp body is partially blended with the entire urban fabric of the city, where there is no physical boundary between the camp and the surrounding neighborhoods, as is notable in the case of Palestinian refugee camps in Jordan. Figure 1.7 presents views toward the camp from Amman.

A researcher, consultant, and teaching fellow in social sciences, urbanism, migration, and refugee camps described his visit to Al-Hussin camp in Amman, in 2020, the capital of Jordan, which is located near the city center, Amman downtown, or as it is known by local Ammanis Al-Balad, as:

> "......After looking at its location on a map, I headed toward the camp, walking up and down the hills of the city, crossing several neighborhoods full of the small cubic houses with their white, grey, and yellow tones that are typical of Amman. When I arrived at the point where the map showed one of the boundaries of the camp, I felt confused. Where I was expecting a clear-cut demarcation between the city and the camp, there was none. In fact, I was not exactly sure where the boundary lies and whether I had entered the camp or not. It was true that the streets had suddenly narrowed, the density of the built-up environment was greater, while the average size of the houses was smaller, and the finished quality of the constructions seemed poorer. Nevertheless, the contrast between the camp and the surrounding city neighborhoods was not as striking as one might have expected....... and its materiality had blended with that of the city. It had clearly undergone a process of urban development".

Every society in history has a specific space that responds to its social and economic needs. Agora was populated only by free male citizens, reflecting its own time's social and political culture. So public space continues to be the political and social barometer of a community. This could also be reflected on the refugee community within the camp space where the camp space is changing based on the refugees' social and economic needs, and in this way, the transformation in the refugee camp could be considered as a barometer that marks and measures the relationship characteristics between the new settlement and the existing city. As Agier said (2002), "Due

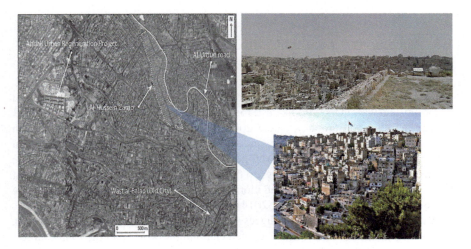

Fig. 1.7 Views taken for Jabal Al-Hussin zone from Amman citadel. Ref: Own illustration 2020

to their very heterogeneity, camps may become the genesis of unexpected cities, new social environment, relationships, and identification."

In fact, under any circumstance, the refugee camps are not planned to last (Osech, 2010). However, the transformation of refugee camps into city-like spaces, especially in the cases of protracted displacement is notable in different contexts all over the world. Examples are in Africa (AsIlcan et al., 2015; Kaiser, 2005, Ilcan et al., 2015; Betts et al., 2015, Perouse de Montclos and Kagwanja, 2000; Agier, 2002; Herz, 2013; Jansen, 2018), the Middle East (Doraï, 2010; Ramadan, 2013; Sanyal, 2014; Abourahme, 2015; Dalal, 2015; Katz, 2015; Martin, 2015; Darling, 2017; Woroniecka-Krzyzanowska, 2017), South Asia (Redclift, 2013; Goreau-Ponceaud, 2014), and Europe (Picker and Pasquetti, 2015; Sigona, 2015; Maestri and Hughes, 2017). It is undoubtedly that those temporary settlements—considering the time factor—are destined to grow with a permeant character in a rapid transformation on its urban, environmental, social, cultural, and economic features. Even though no one (whether the United Nations, host communities, or even the refugees themselves) wants a permanent character for refugee camps, the bitter and definite truth is that they last years, decades, and sometimes for generations (Dunn, 2015). For example, the Palestinians are now getting in their 70 years in exile, the Somalians are entering their 27 years of displacement, and the Syrians have been suffering since 2012. Until now, no one knows the time of return if at all.

Notably, those provisional settlements are expanding, and they are not freezing to the status of their inception. Let us consider one of the latest refugees' settlements in Jordan, the Zaatari refugee camp, which was opened on July 28, 2012, as a result of the Syrian civil war. The camp was formally instituted approximately in the middle of nowhere in a very desolate area. It is 12 km from the Syrian border, around 10 km east of the town of Mafraq, and 45 km north of the capital Amman (Jauhiainen & Vorobeva, 2018).

1.3 Jordan and Zaatari Camp

Jordan has been one of the most notable countries hosting refugees for many years. The country is considered a haven for people forced to flee their countries because of instability and wars in the Middle East. Jordan is strategically located at the crossroads of Asia, Africa, and Europe (Mathew, 2002). Hence, the political situation of Jordan is considered the most stable, safe, and secure environment in the middle east that making Jordan a good choice for refugees who were seeking a safe haven. There are many refugees within Jordan due to the Arab–Israeli conflict and the invasion of Iraq. Presently, Syrians have joined along with Palestinians and Iraqi refugees due to the civil war in Syria (ORSAM, 2014).

The steep influx of Syrian refugees led to the establishment of Zaatari camp. Zaatari camp is the second-largest refugee camp in the world and the fourth largest city in Jordan (Ledwith & Smith, 2014). Figure 1.8 illustrates the location of Zaatari camp in Jordan.

1.3 Jordan and Zaatari Camp

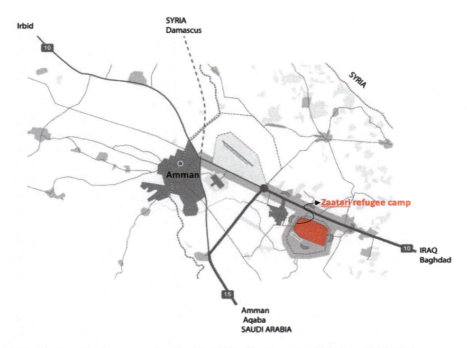

Fig. 1.8 Zaatari refugee camp location. Ref: Edited by the author 2020 from VNG 2016

The United Nations High Commissioner for Refugees (UNHCR) reported around 658,000 total active registered Syrian refugees in Jordan as of August 2020. In comparison, the total refugee population inside the Zaatari camp is 77,479 (UNHCR, 2020a, 2020b, 2020c, 2020d).

Since July 2012, Zaatari has developed from an empty land of desert into a home for around 100.000 people (UNHCR, 2017).

The camp includes 8500 acres of land. As 6700 acres of this land is owned by the Jordanian Armed Forces, and 1800 is owned by industrial cities institution. The Hashemite Charity Organization also rented the two pieces of land to institute the Zaatari refugee camp (Jordanzad, 2013). The camp land is surrounded by an 8.3 km ring road, where the formal layout of the camp is a grid system with two types of structures: caravan prefabricated modular dwelling and tents (UNHCR, 2013). As of December 2013, Zaatari included 17.000 residential caravans, 8000 tents, and 3000 shops (Khandaji & Makawi, 2013). By 2020 the camp has 32 schools, 58 community centers, and 120 mosques spread all over the camp (UNHCR, 2020a, b, c, d). It also has two hospitals with 55 beds and nine health care centers, one delivery unit, and 120 community health volunteers. The camp is famous of its main market street, which is known by the Syrian refugees as "Cham-Elysees," that includes different shops, vegetables kiosks, butchers, clothing stores, and restaurants (Tran, 2013).

Zaatari camp has developed rapidly to accommodate more than 76,143 Syrian refugees (UNHCR, 2020a, b, c, d), which roughly equals an average Jordanian city population. Zaatari population size is remarkably changing because of two main factors: the first factor is the natural growth rate that depends on the birth and death ratios. Zaatari witnesses daily more than 13–15 births (Ibrahim, 2013). The second factor is the continuous decampment of those who are seeking safety far from disastrous events as the camp had received 1500 refugees every night who crossed the borders seeking protection (UNHCR, 2012). When Zaatari camp was officially opened in 2012, the aim was to accommodate around 30,000 Syrian now the camp, which was instituted as a temporary shelter is now considered the fourth largest city in Jordan (Mcghee, 2017). As Fig. 1.9 shows the development of the Zaatari camp since it's institution in 2012 up to 2016.

The camp covers 5.3 km^2 with 24,000 prefabricated caravans (Reliefweb, 2017; UNHCR, 2017). The desert is growing from bare land to a city, and what started as temporary sheltering is now having a definite character of the permanent city. The establishment of the Zaatari refugee camp has been impacting the whole region around. According to Zaatari Municipality, the built-up area of the Zaatari Region has increased by 60% since 2013. Even though the area of the camp is not extendable anymore, the camp is solidifying and integrating with the current spatial configuration.

Jordan also has been hosting refugees since the Arab–Israeli War in 1948, followed by the Six-Day War of 1967 and the Palestinian Intifada in 1987. Now, Jordan has more than 2 million registered Palestine refugees live in ten recognized Palestine refugee camps across the country, and they are (Amman New camp (1955), Baqa'a Camp (1967), Husn Camp (1968), Irbid Camp (1951), Jabal Al-Hussein Camp

Fig. 1.9 Development of the Zaatari refugee camp in northern Jordan, 2012–2016. Map modified from geodata UNITAR/UNOSAT (2016)

1.3 Jordan and Zaatari Camp

(1952), Jerash Camp (1968), Marka Camp (1968), Souf Camp (1967), Talbieh Camp (1968), Zarqa Camp (1949) which accommodate 18% of the country total (UNRWA, 2020). Figure 1.10 shows the difference between the initial and current population for both the Palestinians and Syrian refugee camps in Jordan.

All of the Palestine refugee camps in Jordan are considered protracted based on UNHCR (2004), which defined a protracted refugee situation as a situation in which at least 25,000 refugees from the same country find themselves in exile for more than five consecutive years. Palestine refugees in Jordan have been living in a long-lasting and intractable state of limbo in the refugee camps for more than 70 years. As the Fig. 1.11 tracked the refugee camps in Jordan, the date of their institution and their current conditions.

In Jordan, there are two types of transformation in the refugee camp settlements: The protracted "Palestine refugee camps," which are partially blended in the urban tissue, and have a strong relationship with their neighborhoods as it could be seen in Al-Wehdat camp and Al-Hussin camp, and others. The second one is the reshaping of the temporary character of the camp space (building material, services, density) of the camp settlement within its borders as an isolated island which exemplifies the temporary status city within the camp boundaries with no proper relationship with the surrounding built environment as in Zaatari refugee camp and Al-Azraq camp.

For instance, Amman's new camp which is locally recognized as "Al-Wehdat" was instituted by the United Nations Relief and Work Agency for Palestine refugees in the near east "UNRWA" in 1955 to provide shelter for the Palestinian refugees after 1948 Arab–Israeli war is now one of the most important commercial hubs of the eastern Ammanis where there are around 2500 markets over an area of 0.48 km^2 (UNRWA, 2019a, b). As seen in Fig. 1.12 the camp context in numbers.

Al-Wehdat camp which is located in the heart of Amman city. Amman, as other Mediterranean cities, has its peculiar characteristics since Amman has a deep history,

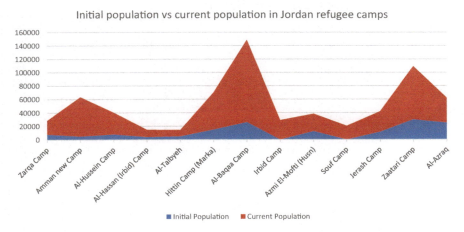

Fig. 1.10 Initial population verses current camps population in the refugee camps in Jordan. By the author 2020 from UNRWA (2019a, 2019b)/UNHCR 2019

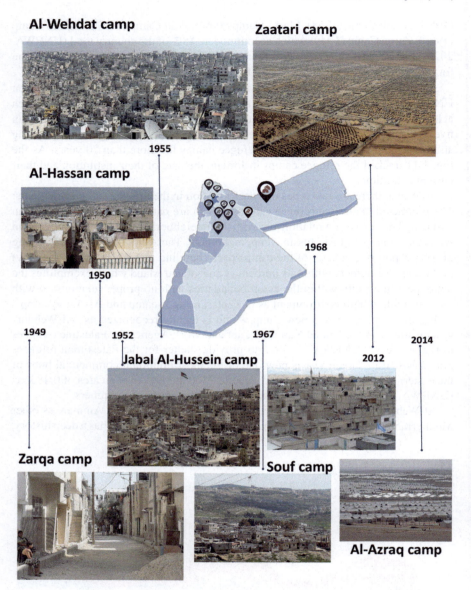

Fig. 1.11 The transformation of the refugee camps in Jordan to permanent cities. By the author 2020

1.3 Jordan and Zaatari Camp

The Camp area	**0.48 km^2**
Population	58311
Population density	121734.8
Numbers of Families	12630
Number of residential units	2130
Number of families in one Residential unit	6
Number of security center	1
Number of post offices	1
Number of bakeries	10
Number of Mosques	7
Number of Pharmacies	8
Number of Markets	2500
Number of clubs	1
Number of schools	16
Number of kindergartens	5
Number of clinic centers	3
Number of private clinics	22

Fig. 1.12 Amman New Camp context. By the author 2019 From UNRWA (2019a, b)

especially the east of Amman, which is rich in different historical sights. For instance, Al-Wehdat camp is surrounded by various historical landmarks of the city of Amman, like the Roman amphitheater, Roman Nymphaeum, and Amman Citadel. As seen in Fig. 1.13.

The hazardous way in which the camp has transformed into a permanent part of the urban fabric has shaped a very deteriorated urban image because the camp blended partially with the surrounding context as a result of the Amman urban growth. Despite the fact, the camp residents are dreaming of their return as its clear from the name of the camps quarter (Al-Awdeh) which means "the return," that indicates to the refugee's hope of return is still alive, but in the same way, the rhythm of life needs permanent solutions. Any kind of settlement needs to deeply analyze and synthesize the context to not disturbing its historical sedimentation of time. Now Al-Wehdat is the commercial hub for many of the eastern Amman residents, where banks, jewelers,

Fig. 1.13 Main landmarks in Amman New Camp zone. By the author 2019

pharmacies, travel agencies, appliance and electronic shops, and a vast number of groceries, clothing stores, and vegetable shops (Hammarneh, 2019).

Consequently, the inevitable fact is that there is a great need for an urban planning project capable of working on the form of settlements, concerning the "time" dimension. Time must be managed in the space project to have a good result as an urban environment—both within the so-called temporary settlement and in the relationship with the existing city, of which the new field will undoubtedly become part of the city urban fabric. What we need to understand is that reconstruction today concerns increasingly complex urban realities, which is always a very long process—longer than what we are led to imagine each time. This process typically involves several generations; from it, a new society will certainly be born that will have a strong link with the territory and with the host city.

On the one hand, the new generations born in the fields will express a growing need for a city and definitive urban quality. This phenomenon is very similar to what we can see in the suburbs of our cities and metropolises, in the slums as in the settlements that arise, without government, on the margins of the southern cities. On the other hand, cities are living organisms that are sensitive to any transformation taking place in their territory. We are getting used to thinking of cities as static objects, but this is an inappropriate vision because the urban territory is always a unitary organism: a body with senses, a breath, and a capacity for reaction. Even if the construction processes were short, the refugee camps would produce permanent changes to the skin of the cities. However, the construction processes are always long, so it is necessary to change the point of view and to look not only at the arrangement of the "temporary" field but in the whole city. It is essential to imagine the city's future also in terms of how the existence of this new part will influence it.

In summary, time is a decisive factor in refugee camps because it could be discussed in terms of two points of interest: the construction time of these provisional settlements and the length of stay for both the refugees and the camp in the hosting country. The concept of speedy construction during an emergency is a critical issue, in that different stakeholders are seeking to implement swift solutions to provide lodging for refugees within a short period, while neglecting the fact that any type of construction requires time and creating settlements for a mass exodus of refugees is utterly different from preparing a military camp or summer camp, which has provisional activities. Turning a blind eye to the construction time will lead to poorly or hastily built environments with materials of poor quality, which will shape a provisional character into refugee camps and provide refugees with minimum living conditions. Thinking and dealing with refugee camps in a "three-dimensional" way is not a solution anymore since time—which is the fourth dimension—plays a vital role in reforming provisional settlements into more permanent cities. A refugee crisis can turn into an urban mess because the refugees who are living in tentative cities over a long period are reformulating an urban mark on the city's image while annihilating its infrastructure, services, and economy (Baeumler et al., 2017). While refugee camps have all the characteristics which shape a city, they are still planned tentatively.

1.4 Syria and Damascus City

The Syrian Arab Republic is located on the east coast of the Mediterranean Sea in southwestern Asia (Scullard, 2021). Syria borders Jordan to the south, Palestine and Lebanon to the southwest, Turkey to the north, and Iraq to the east and southeast (Gammer, 2004) as shown in Fig. 1.14. Damascus is the capital of the Syrian Arab republic. Since the second millennium BCE, Damascus has been an active commercial center, and it went through different stages of urbanization. Damascus encountered massive growth during the second half of the twentieth century due to the youth migration from rural areas seeking jobs and better living conditions (Rabbat, 2021).

Since the beginning of the Syrian Civil War in 2011, the armed conflict in Syria had produced disastrous repercussions on the Syrian population, the country's infrastructure, and economy (The German Institute for International and Security Affairs "SWP", 2020).

According to the United Nations, the Syrian conflict shaped the largest migrant and refugee crisis since World War II. More than half of Syria's pre-war population of twenty-two million has been displaced internally or to neighboring countries such

Fig. 1.14 The location of the Syrian Arab Republic. Ref: https://www.cfr.org/article/syrias-civil-war

as Jordan, Lebanon, and Turkey (Scullard, 2021). In 2022, there are 6.6 million Syrian refugees in the world right now (UNHCR, 2022). The conflict in Syria has generated great destruction on Syria's infrastructure, the energy and housing sector, health and educational institutions, and agricultural lands. The most harmful damage concentrated in contested areas as the eastern suburbs of Damascus, the Yarmouk refugee camp at the southern periphery of the capital, the East of Aleppo, Al-Raqqa, Homs, and Hama (SWP, 2020). Although the armed conflict was in surrounding areas of the capital, Damascus' urban fabric and social structure paid the highest cost. The majority of homes in the Eastern and Southeastern fringe of the city were destroyed or severely damaged; meanwhile, other parts of Damascus city have received nearly a million internally displaced persons who fled from different parts of the Syrian territory (Ibrahim & Wind, 2020).

1.5 How Cities Absorb and Deal with the Sudden Population Influx and the Need for Urban Housing?

In some cases, and as a result of emergency events whether natural incidents such as (earthquakes, hurricanes, tornados.... etc.), or human-made disasters such as (wars, conflicts, or any terrorism action) cities face a sudden abnormal influx of people who are in an urgent need for housing. This issue represents an enormous burden on city planners and urban politics to tackle the urgent need for housing and to cope with the refugees and the internally displaced persons "IDPs" pressure on infrastructure and essential services.

Evidently, cities tend to deal with the sudden demand for housing of the displaced population within three main approaches: The first provides temporary transitional housing in a full housing project, such as the C.A.S.E project in L'Aquila, Italy, after the earthquake of April 6, 2009. The second approach uses the concept of alternative housing (empty residential buildings, clusters of apartments, or independent urban apartments), as observed in the case of Thessaloniki, Greece. The third approach employs constructing emergency shelters and refugee camps, as in the Jordanian scenario dealing with Palestinian and Syrian refugees.

1.5.1 The C.A.S.E Project in L'Aquila—The Abruzzo Region—Italy

To provide emergency settlements within a short period does not mean temporary material, provisional character, or "makeshift cities." As mentioned previously, the city of L'Aquila in the Abruzzo region dealt with emergency displacement as a result of the 2009 earthquake. The city planners succeeded in constructing a residential city within only six months from the earthquake using light structure but destined to be part of the new city.

L'Aquila exposed to a terrible earthquake with a magnitude of 5.9—on the Richter scale—on 6 April 2009 (Ray, 2018), which extensively damaged the whole city. The earthquake made around 70.000 people homeless who were temporarily accommodated in tented camps or hotels. In September 2009, the government launched a project called "C.A.S.E," which means "Homes," which, by August 2010, offered a settlement for more than 15.000 persons (Frate, 2017). And by 2013, L'Aquila had recovered almost all the displaced persons—70,000—and the tented camps had already been removed.

The C.A.S.E. project provided the displaced persons with durable settlements, which are neither temporary nor definitive, nor rather the two things together. The project focused on delivering the earthquake victims with housing solutions that could last for a long time until they return to their homes of origin. Once that happens, the new settlements will be opened for university students or tourists. Over seven months from May to December 2009, the construction cycle finished from planning to houses handovers, the project did not provide the people with prefabricated caravans but wooden houses, there are also (25–30) typical apartments, developed on three floors with a base of (12 × 48 m) (Tozzi, 2009). The so-called "New Villages" are configured as assemblages of residential complexes, surrounded by a multipurpose center for services and, in many cases, with a beautiful overlooking to the landscape.

The buildings are typical in size and type, changing their appearance and materials according to the company that makes them: the new settlements have railing or balconies, with prefabricated elements in wood, concrete, or coated metal structures. They have a large, robust, concrete, solid foundations designed to protect the residents in case of seismic events. Still, also, they serve as a car park with varying capacity of about 35 vehicles (Tozzi, 2009) according to the building size and type, creating thus an essential module for urban planning.

The "houses of tomorrow" is the central concept which addressed the C.A.S.E project with a clear vision of a city for the future, a construction system which designed and built a total of 5 complexes for a total of 135 housing units in less than 80 days with innovative and environmentally-friendly techniques. It built sustainable and anti-seismic settlements that provided thermal comfort and energy saving with high thermal insulations in walls and roofs, which reduced the thermal consumption up to 10 kWh/m^2 per year that also helped in reducing heating and cooling costs. The new settlement units were designed with large openings that provide natural light, ventilation, and keep the population connected with the nature around them. The decision to use wood as a building material helps in creating ideal spaces where people could live, work, study, and spend free time in contact with context. As shown in Fig. 1.15.

A plan of (12 × 48 m) for the housing unit is a place where one can live, not an incubator of 45 m^2, a place with architectural quality, suitable materials, energy efficiency, and environmental sustainability. The project created new urbanizations of widespread settlements in areas out of the Municipality Master Plan, which is not new urban fabric but an extension to what already exists.

Fig. 1.15 L'Aquila C.A.S.E project. Ref. News-town, 2016

The new emergency settlements generated a profound modification on the city's territorial structure from a centripetal model, almost wholly centered on the ancient nucleus of the city to a linear trend in which the city has been reorganized abided by the running road from east to west. The project sought to find new centrality to the core of the "C.A.S.E" project with the peripheral nuclei, which existed before the earthquake of 2009. The city that has been formed and which is consolidating by time will soon reveal an essential demand for better urban quality as it will absorb most of the available resources.

Generally, the practical intervention during the emergency in L'Aquila showed an excellent response to provide aid and support for the stricken people not only in providing accommodation but also to sustainably fulfil the residents' needs. The response was very quick with a perspective on future development, a lesson to be learned from L'Aquila, a village that was assumed to be temporary but more than seven years, and it is still functioning very well. L'Aquila's people are now living in a "temporary status" because they will go back to their homes, but they are not living in a "temporary city."

1.5.2 An Adequate Urban Housing for Refugees in the Thessaloniki-Greece

Thessaloniki is known by Greeks as the "Mother of Migration," because it has been hosting refugees since the Sephardic Jews in the 1400 s up to now. Thessaloniki provides a safe haven to refugees and asylum seekers from Syria, Afghanistan, Iraq, Turkey, South Asia, and Africa (Kasra et al., 2020). Thessaloniki is a mid-size city situated in northern Greece, on Thermaikos Bay, part of the Aegean Sea. It is the second-largest city in Greece, with 324,766 inhabitants. Thessaloniki is the most important center of the metropolitan area since it is considered to have direct influence over the whole region of Central Macedonia. Built near the sea (50 km of the coastal front), it Makes Thessaloniki a home to the country's second-largest export and transit port and the nearest European Union port to the Balkans and Black Sea zone (URBACT, 2021). The location of Thessaloniki on the Balkans Route makes it the second or third stop for asylum seekers traveling irregularly to Northern Europe after crossing from Turkey. The city is a destination for many refugees and asylum seekers because of its significant international humanitarian attitude and existing smugglers. They assist the irregular migrants in moving to North Macedonia or Bulgaria to other cities, promoting better opportunities like Germany (Kasra et al., 2020).

The refugee camps in the Northern regions of Greece such as Cherso, Veria, and Deverni accommodate around 13,000 refugees (Kasra et al., 2020), the camp itself remains a short-term housing response until the borders were closed in March 2016. Figure 1.16 demonstrates Diavata camp in Thessaloniki in Greece.

After March 2016, the main housing program in Thessaloniki funded by UNHCR, come up with different housing proposals such as hotel rooms (UNHCR), hosting in

Fig. 1.16 Diavata camp, Thessaloniki-Greece. Ref: Refugee Studies Centre, Oxford Department of International Development, University of Oxford, 2020

1.5 How Cities Absorb and Deal with the Sudden Population Influx …

Greek families (Solidarity Now), rental of individual apartments in the city (PRAXIS, ARSIS), or collective apartment buildings (Solidarity Now, CRS). By November 2016, this entire program has accommodated about 1600 people (Deprez & Labattut, 2016). See in Table 1.2 the accommodation alternatives for the refugees in Thessaloniki.

In Thessaloniki, only 1% of the accommodation alternatives are emergency shelters, while the most favorable option was the use of the apartments as alternative housing for refugees with ratio reaches 71% and rehabilitated apartments 38%. There were also other choices including community buildings 7% and hotels 3%. As illustrated in Fig. 1.17.

The Norwegian Refugee Council (NRC) developed a proposal with four different scenarios to provide better accommodation alternatives for the refugees in Thessaloniki, which called "adequate housing for refugees." The project aimed to meet the refugees' needs with descent standards that foster their integration within the city of Thessaloniki. As shown in Fig. 1.18.

Table 1.2 Accommodation alternatives for the refugees in Thessaloniki

Organization	Type of accommodation	Number of places	Number of families	Other services
UNHCR	Hotel	58		Day center
	Host families	110		
	Apartments		11	
	Emergency shelter	30	11	
Solidarity Now	Apartments	129	25	Shelters for: unaccompanied minors, homeless and Asylum seeker.
PRAXIS	Apartments	267	60	Polyclinic & Day center
Municipality of Thessaloniki	Host families	15	4	
	Apartments	235	42	
	Community buildings	28	7	
CRS	Buildings	250		
Iliaktida	Apartments	250	60	
Iliachtida	Apartments	600	190	
Actual UNHCR Accommodation Program Capacity				
Housing Project	Apartments	150		
Elpida	Community buildings	127		Different activities inside the building
Oikopolis	Rehabilitated apartments	38		Day center
Filoxena	Community buildings		30	

Ref: By the author 2020 from Deprez and Labattut (2016)

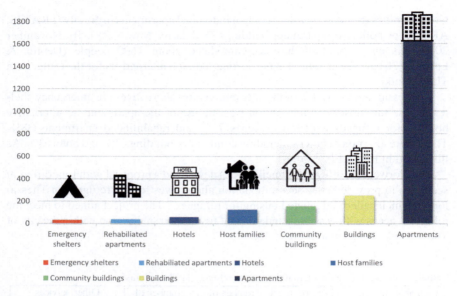

Fig. 1.17 Accommodation alternatives in Thessaloniki. Ref: by the author 2020

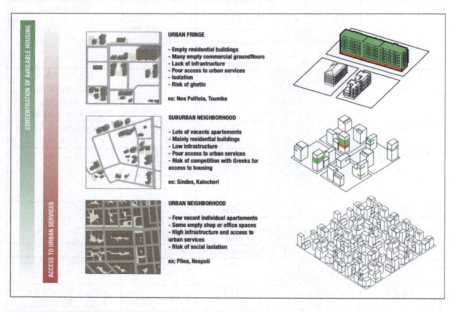

Fig. 1.18 Typologies of housing opportunities and urban fabric in Thessaloniki. Ref: Norwegian Refugee Center project 2016

The NRC study reviewed Thessaloniki history; it analyzed its urban context and discussed the Greek crisis, especially in the sector of housing and tenure. The study found that there are three main available housing typologies: Vacant buildings, individual apartments already on the rental market, and groups or concentrations of apartments in specific neighborhoods.

The study came up with four main scenarios for the main opportunities of refugees housing relocation based on the available housing typologies, the status of the people to be accommodated, and the service-related assistance and type of follow-up required.

- The first scenario requires an identification of the empty residential buildings to rehouse a large number of refugees in the underserved areas on the urban fringes of the metropolitan areas within an integrated approach.
- The second scenario seeks to provide a broader range of accommodation types for the relocated people. That has average access to public services and transport, to help the refugees in creating new social relationships, to be highly connected and integrated with the surrounding neighborhoods, and to abide by the provision of the services for the vulnerable communities.
- The third scenario would provide individual apartments in well-served areas to more self-sufficient people, and enhance their access to services with regular follow up.
- The fourth scenario focuses on emergency cases in urgent need of housing out-of-camps and homeless people. The first step is to open an emergency center that connected with health services and can be used to lodge people for short-term stays (one to two weeks) before their referral to longer-term housing solutions.

Assessing the available buildings to accommodate refugees is an essential step to provide sufficient housing solutions with no use of temporary emergency shelters, especially during the reconstruction process. The displaced persons could temporarily live in such an alternative until a permanent city is built.

1.5.3 The Refugee Camps as an Alternative—Jordan

Historically, refugees' camps as a response for unpredicted population influx are not a contemporary phenomenon; they were used in Rome to accommodate the inhabitants from unexpected Tiber river's floods in "Campus Martius" (Hailey, 2009). The refugee camp was defined in UNHCR policy as special zones with specific characteristics to provide secure and safe environments where refugees can live and do their own business (UNHCR, 2013). According to Gale (2008) refugee camps are short-term living solutions managed by the host government and non-governmental organizations (NGOs) to provide lodging, education, health, and hygiene services to the refugee community. These units come in different shapes and light structures like tents, huts, or car box living structures. Agamben (2008) described the quintessence of refugee camps as the "materialization of the state of exception."

The refugee camps vary according to their size, shape, and life span. Some refugee settlements constructed to lodge around 50 people like the settlements for the Sri Lankan refugees in India; other camps accommodated more than 150.000 people such as Burundi refugees in Tanzania (Magrinà, 2006). Refugee camps also have a different life span, as an example, the Palestinian refugee camps, which last more than 65 years. As (Bauman, 2001) said that "If common consent and history books establish the seventeenth century as the age of reason, the eighteenth century as the age of enlightenment and the nineteenth century as the age of revolutions, the best name to describe the twentieth century is the age of camps."

Jordan considered a recently established nation but did not make use of architecture and urbanism during the nation-building process. To put in evidence, Amman, the capital of Jordan, is a city that was shaped mostly by migration waves and organically sculpted by refugees. Refugees and migrants gave shape to the cityscapes and the urban scenery.

Jordan is a case in point of how refugee camps stand for decades and are being transformed into permanent cities (Alshoubaki & Zazzara, 2020). Jordan is strategically located in the heart of the Arab world. Since its independence in 1946, it has undergone various waves of displacement since the Arab–Israeli War in 1948, followed by the Six-Day War of 1967 and the Palestinian Intifada in 1987. Recently, in 2012, Jordan received a massive exodus of Syrian refugees because of the Syrian Civil War (The Center for Middle Eastern Strategic Studies [ORSAM], 2014). Accordingly, Jordan has around 15 refugee camps ranging from 6 years old up to 70 years. See the basic data about the refugee camps in data in Table 1.3 and their distribution in Fig. 1.19.

During the last five decades, the population of Jordan had increased ten times, see Fig. 1.20, part of this rapid growth due to natural increase and immigration from rural areas, while the real reason is political, as mentioned previously (Al-Daly, 2020). The statistical data suggest that the Jordan population has multiplied six-fold during the period 1952–1995. Amman has grown massively in a short space of time (Meaton & Alnsour, 2012), the population growth in Amman remains on the rise, growing from 90,000 in 1950 to 2,148,000 in 2020 (UN, 2020). Amman population has been multiplied 24-fold within 70 years. The population growth is utterly the most influential factor in generating profound modification on the cities' urban fabric and a clear contributor in creating their urban scenery.

The sprawling camps in Jordan, are ringing urgent alarms to change the conception of refugee camps as temporary cities since they last long periods and because of their prolonged existence take a permanent character in terms of material, expansion, urban economic, and spatial layout resulting in a profound impact on the urban tissue around them. The shift occurring on those provisional settlements must be reflected with an urban eye in shifting the policies of dealing with such kind of phenomena. The issue of refugee camp planning required from planners, architects, and emergency managers to think from the beginning and in the preliminary stages of emergency in the organization and the expansion of those temporary settlements.

The refugee camps scenario in Jordan requires planners to reimagine and to rethink these provisional cities since their inception as probable permanent cities able to get

Table 1.3 Basic data about the refugee camps in Jordan

	Institution date	Area (Km^2)	Initial population	Current population	Population density	Residential units (No.)
Zarqa camp	1949	0.182	8000	20,316	0.11	1135
Amman New camp	1955	0.479	5000	58,311	0.12	2130
Al-Hussein camp	1952	0.445	8000	32,217	0.07	2488
Al-Hassan (Irbid) camp	1950	0.961	4000	10,500	0.01	648
Al-Talbyeh	1968	0.133	5000	9354	0.07	810
Hittin camp (Marka)	1968	0.894	15,000	54,876	0.06	2824
Al-Baqaa camp	1968	0.148	26,000	122,579	0.82	8507
Irbid camp	1950	0.234	–	28,690	0.12	1660
Azmi El-Mofti (Husn)	1968	0.758	12,500	25,776	0.03	2314
Souf camp	1967	0.534	–	20,097	0.03	1179
Jerash camp	1968	0.531	11,500	30,379	0.05	2130
Zaatari camp	2012	5.3	30,000	78,994	0.01	25,815
Al-Azraq	2014	1.47	25,000	36,705	0.02	10,479

Own illustration from UNRWA and UNHCR 2020

in profound transformation and development toward more creative, flexible, and dynamic cities. It is essential to focus on their co-existence within the surrounding neighborhoods because their destiny is to be sooner or later part of this urban tissue, and that was proved by experience and history. As United Nations High Commissioner for Refugees Filippo Grandi said: "Inclusion is the name of the game" (Katz, 2017). Those "temporary cities" must be highly integrated within the urban tissue, and that requires, again, to plan camps as cities from the beginning. The enrollment of architects and urban planners is essential in the preliminary stages of emergency to prepare comprehensive studies to the "New-born" cities, to assess their location, to sustainably plan them with appropriate methods, techniques, considering the context and the surrounding urban fabric. The temporary "canvas cities" keep people alive but without proper living conditions.

Promoting new strategic plans for those new spaces, able to develop new economies, would be of great benefit for hosting countries. According to the World Bank, Zaatari refugee camp, for example, costs around $500,000 per day to run (Smith, 2014), but what is the maximum end value? Refugees are still passive aid receivers even though they have skills, abilities, and qualifications: an essential source of economic growth for hosting countries if provided with a proper environment.

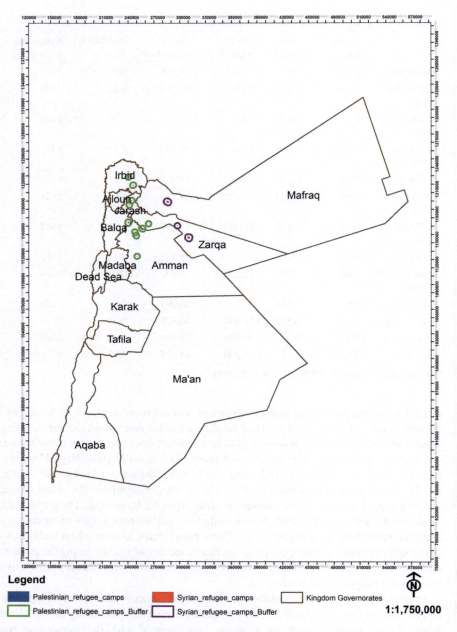

Fig. 1.19 The distribution of the refugee camps in Jordan. By the author 2019

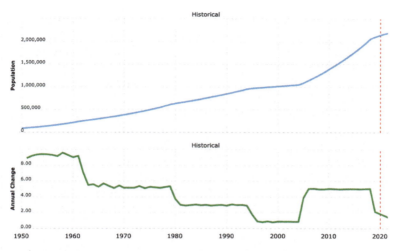

Fig. 1.20 The population growth of Amman from 1950 to 2020. Ref: UN, 2020

Outlining a comprehensive urban planning theme will produce a balance between refugees' needs and host communities' potentials. It could be attained by following a bottom-up approach that highly seeks to involve the displaced persons during all stages of an emergency, from the preliminary assessment of their needs and aspirations to their active participation in building their new cities. The planning must consider the local context for opportunities, threats, strengths, and weaknesses with a clear vision of future developments.

Refugees need permanent settlements, not just shelter, to live in homes, not in incubators, to have cities, not prisons, to be integrated not marginalized, and to become self-sufficient, not dependents. At the same time, host communities need real cities, not slums, a peaceful environment not to bring conflict, to have a clean environment not to generate pollution and diseases, to live in well-planned cities far from any hazardous expansion to their city urban fabric.

1.6 The Structure of the Book

This book is structured in five chapters as following:

- The first chapter: The temporary city: This chapter analyzed the refugee camps as an urban phenomenon, discussing the camp's relation with its neighborhood and the cities' response to the sudden population influx's needs for urgent housing.
- The second chapter: The Urbicide: This chapter discussed the politics of urban destruction in cities, introducing two types of urbicide: the direct urbicide and the indirect urbicide, to develop an integrated spatial planning approach to deal with emergencies.

- The third chapter: Urban emergency integrated planning *UEIP:* This chapter analyzed the direct urbicide in Damascus city in Syria and the indirect urbicide in the Zaatari refugee camp in Jordan, investigating their urban scenario and the governing planning laws and regulations.
- The fourth chapter: Spaces in emergency: This chapter synthesized the Damascus city and the Zaatari refugee camp within the spatial sphere, the diagnostic and assessment sphere, and the construction laws and the technical standards sphere. Proposing an innovative conceptual framework Urban Emergency Integrated Planning—[UEIP] to confront the post-conflict displacement.
- The fifth chapter: *UEIP and FUTURE directions:* This chapter discussed the importance of this study to urban planning and future research. It argued the temporary city hypothesis policy presented by this study and the UEIP framework, which built to respond to emergencies and organize the post-conflict reconstruction.

1.7 Conclusion

The metamorphosis of refugee camps into decaying cities happens due to the continuous increase in the population densities and the physical modifications carried out by the refugees themselves based on their needs, which shape an arbitrary expansion over a long period. Besides, implementing incremental planning strategies in designing the refugee camp settlements based on numbers and minimum standards. This chapter reviewed different refugee camp design standards from various manuals and handbooks, proving that the emergency response works on one size fits all that create temporary cities with low qualities. This chapter concludes that refugees' camps' hazardous transformation leads the cities to the point of no return and non-appeal since migration and displacement shape a real burden on the city's urban structure guides widespread environmental degradation over time, and create informal spaces their conditions between intolerable and catastrophic. Consequently, it brings to light the main idea of this argument: the temporary city hypothesis, which is about the spatial organization that deals with the sudden population in case of displacement, whether internally or out of borders. It helps to understand the transformation of the refugee camps from a very provisional settlement into slum-like neighborhoods.

References

Abourahme, N. (2015). Assembling and spilling-over: towards an 'ethnography of cement' in a Palestinian refugee camp. *International Journal of Urban and Regional Research, 39*(2), 200–17.
Agamben, G. (2008). State of Exception. University of Chicago Press.
Agier, M. (2002). Between war and city towards an urban anthropology of refugee camps, *Ethnography, 3*, 317–341.

References

Al Daly, J. (2020). *Informal settlements in Jordan upgrading approaches adopted and lessons learned*. Retrieved 2020, from: www.hdm.lth.se/fileadmin/hdm/alumni/papers/ad1999/ad1999-09.pdf.

Alshoubaki, H. (2018). The temporary city: The transformation of refugee camps from ... - eiris. Retrieved 12AD, from http://eiris.it/hopue_numeri/hopue_n_7_dicembre_2018/aa1_The_temporary_city_Hind.pdf.

Alshoubaki, H., & Zazzara, L. (2020). The fragility in the land of refugees: Jordan and irrepressible phenomenon of refugee camps. *Journal of International Studies, 13*(1), 123–142. https://doi.org/10.14254/2071-8330.2020/13-1/8

AmmannetTV. (2015). [The Last Passenger] Youtube video. http://www.youtube.com/watch?v=3v3df4XJjpo#t=1183.

Baeumler, A., Shah, & Biau. (2017). Cities of Refuge: Bringing an urban lens to the forced displacement challenge. Retrieved from http://blogs.worldbank.org/sustainablecities/cities-refuge-bringing-urban-lens-forceddisplacement-challenge.

Barqawi. (2014). Patience running out in Jordan after influx of Syrian refugees. The Guardian. Retrieved from https://www.theguardian.com/world/2014/dec/01/jordan-syrian-refugees-patience-running-out.

Bauman, Z. (2001). The century of camps. In P. Beilharz (Ed.), *The Bauman reader* (p. 230). Wiley.

Cattaneo, B. (2020). How our planet became more urbanised than ever. Retrieved from https://ec.europa.eu/jrc/en/news/how-our-planet-became-more-urbanised-ever.

Cuny, F. (1977). Refugee camps and camp planning: The state of the art. *Disasters, 1*(2), 125.

Dalal, A. (2015). A socio-economic perspective on the urbanisation of Zaatari camp in Jordan. *Migration Letters, 12*(3), 263–78.

Darling, J. (2017). Privatising asylum: Neoliberalisation, depoliticisation and the governance of forced migration. *Transactions of the Institute of British Geographers, 41*, 230–243.

D'Ettorre, G. (2016). *Refugee camps: Planning approaches*. Retrieved March 08, 2017, from http://wsimag.com/architecture-and-design/19741-refugee-camps-planning-approaches.

Deprez & Labattut. (2016). Study on Adequate Urban Housing for Refugees in Thessaloniki, Greece. Retrieved https://www.alnap.org/help-library/study-on-adequate-urban-housing-for-refugees-in-thessaloniki-greece.

Doraï, M. K. (2010). Palestinian refugee camps in Lebanon: Migration, mobility and the urbanization process. In A. Knudsen & S. Hanafi (Eds.), *Palestinian refugees: Identity, space and place in the Levant*. Routledge.

Dunn, C. (2015). *The failure of refugee camps*. Retrieved 01/2018, from http://bostonreview.net/editors-picks-world/elizabeth-dunn-failure-refugee-camps.

Earnest, J. (2015). Post-conflict reconstruction—a case study in Kosovo: The complexity of planning and implementing infrastructure projects. *International Journal of Emergency Services, 4*, 103.

Frate. (2017). Casa in Sughero corkpan a Vista Arch frate a Felino. Tecnosugheri. Retrieved 12AD, from https://www.tecnosugheri.it/intervento/villa-sughero-vista-architetto-frate-felino/.

Gale, L. A. (2008). The invisible refugee camp: Durable solutions for boreah 'residuals' in guinea. *Journal of Refugee Studies, 21*(4), 537–552. https://doi.org/10.1093/jrs/fen040

Gammer, M. (Ed.). (2004). *The caspian region, Volume 2: The Caucasus* (1st ed.). Routledge. https://doi.org/10.4324/9780203005125.

Grbac, P. (2013). Civitas, polis, and urbs Reimagining the refugee camp as the city. *Refugee Studies Centre*. https://livedzaatariproject.files.wordpress.com

Hailey, C. (2009). *Camps: a guide to 21st-century space*. Cambridge, Mass.: MIT Press.

Herz, M. (2013). Refugee camps or ideal cities in dust and dirt, in Urban Transformation (Berlin: Ruby Press).

Hammarneh. (2019). Transformation of Al-Wihdat refugee camp. Retrieved 2019, from https://openaccess.leidenuniv.nl/bitstream/handle/1887/16803/ISIM_10_Transformation_of_Al-Wihdat_Refugee_Camp.pdf.

Howard, & Spice. (1973). Plastic sheeting—oxfamilibrary.openrepository.com. Retrieved 12AD, from https://oxfamilibrary.openrepository.com/bitstream/handle/10546/115399/bk-plastic-sheeting-emergency-shelter-010189-en.pdf?sequence=5.

Ibrahim. (2013). Post-War Resettlement and Urban Reconstruction: A case study of Khorram-Shahr, Iran. Retrieved from https://www.researchgate.net/publication/290482002_Post-War_Resettlement_and_Urban_Reconstruction_A_case_study_of_Khorram-Shahr_Iran.

Ilcan, S., Oliver, M., Connoy, L. (2015). Humanitarian assistance and the politics of self-reliance: Uganda's Nakivale refugee settlement. CIGI Policy Brief. Forthcoming.

Jansen, B.J. (2018). *Kakuma refugee camp: humanitarian urbanism in Kenya's accidental city*. Zed Books, London.

Jauhiainen, J., & Vorobeva, E. (2018). Migrants, asylum seekers and refugees in Jordan, 2017. Retrieved 2020, from https://www.researchgate.net/publication/325594771_MIGRANTS_ASYLUM_SEEKERS_AND_REFUGEES_IN_JORDAN_2017.

Jennings, B. (2001). From the urban to the civic: The moral possibilities of the city. *Journal of Urban Health: Bulletin of the New York Academy of Medicine, 78*(1), 88.

Jordanzad. (2013). Zaatari camp institution. Retrieved 12AD, from https://www.jordanzad.com/.

Kasra, M., Mohammad, O., Saad, R., Terzi, I., & Khatri, A. (2020). Thessaloniki, Greece: A Case Report in Refugees in Towns-Tufts-Feinstein International Center. Retrieved from https://fic.tufts.edu/publication-item/to-integrate-or-to-move-on-a-case-study-of-refugees-in-towns/.

Katz, I. (2015). Spreading and concentrating: The camp as the space of the frontier. *City, 19*(5), 727–740.

Katz, I. (2017). Between bare life and everyday life: Spatialising Europe's migrant camps. *Amps: Architecture_Media_Politics_Society (UCL Press)*.

Kennedy, J. (2008). *Structures for the displaced: Service and identity in refugee settlements*. International Forum of Urbanism.

Khandaji, H., & Makawi, M. (2013). 54,000 Syrians Bribe Their Way to Escape Zaatari Camp. *Arab Reporters for Investigative Journalism*, December 4. http://arij.net/en/54000-syrians-bribe-their-way-escape-zaatari-camp.

Kleinschmidt, K. (2015). Interview by conner maher. January. Zaatari Refugee Camp, Jordan.

Koop, A. (2021). Mapped: Where are the world's ongoing conflicts today? Visual Capitalist. Retrieved December 29, 2021, from https://www.visualcapitalist.com/mapped-where-are-the-worlds-ongoing-conflicts-today/.

Ledwith, A., & Smith, D. (2014). Zaatari: The Instant City (Rep.). An Affordable Housing Institute Publication. Retrieved from: http://sigus.scripts.mit.edu/x/files/Zaatari/AHIPublication.pdf.

Legeby, A. (2010). *Urban Segregation And Urban Form From residential segregation to segregation in public space* (Master's thesis, Stockholm-Sweden, 2010). Stockholm: KTH Royal Institute of Technology Architecture and the Built Environment.

MacCallum, D., Babb, C., & Curtis, C. (2019). *Doing research in urban and regional planning: Lessons in practical methods*. Routledge.

Maestri, G. & Hughes S. M. (2017). Contested spaces of citizenship: Camps, borders and urban encounters. *Citizenship Studies, 21*(6), 625–39.

Magrinà, L. (2006). *Refugees in the 21st century, can we find a solution?* The Jesuit Refugee Service (JRS). Retrieved from https://www.cristianismeijusticia.net/files/en123.

Maqusi, S. (2014). 'Space of refuge': Negotiating space with refugees inside the Palestinian camp. MDPI. Retrieved from https://www.mdpi.com/2076-0787/6/3/60.

Martin, D., Minca, C., & Katz, I. (2015). Rethinking the camp: On spatial technologies of power and resistance. Progress in Human Geography. https://doi.org/10.1177/0309132519856702.

Mathew. (2002). The rough guide to Jordan (Vol. 1). Rough Guides.

McGhee, A. (2017). *Life inside the refugee shelter that's now Jordan's fourth largest city*. Retrieved 2020, from http://www.abc.net.au/news/2017-07-28/zaatari-refugee-camp/8749866.

Meaton, J., & Alnsour, J. (2012). Spatial and environmental planning challenges in amman. *Jordan, Planning Practice & Research, 27*(3), 367–386. https://doi.org/10.1080/02697459.2012.673321

Montclos, M-A. P. D., & Kagwanja, P. M. (2000) Refugee camps or cities? The socio-economic dynamics of the Dadaab and Kakuma camps in Northern Kenya. *Journal of Refugee Studies, 13*(2), 205–222.

References

Oesch, L. (2010). *The evolution of urban upgrading and rehabilitation in greater Amman*. Retrieved 2020, from https://www.academia.edu/3268767/The_Evolution_of_Urban_Upgrading_and_Rehabilitation_in_Greater_Amman.

ORSAM. (2014). Effects of the Syrian refugees in Turkey. ORSAM report No 195 (Ankara: ORSAM). https://www.orsam.org.tr/.

Pasquetti, S. (2015). Negotiating control: Camps, cities and political life. *City, 19*(5), 702–713.

Pawar, A., Epstein, C. R., & Simon, S. C. (2015). Emergency management and social intelligence: a comprehensive all-hazards approach.

Picker, G., & Pasquetti, S. (2015). Durable camps: the state, the urban, the everyday: Introduction. *City, 19*(5): 681–688.

Rabbat, N. O. (2021). *Damascus. Encyclopedia Britannica.* https://www.britannica.com/place/Damascus.

Ramadan, A. (2013). Spatialising the refugee camp. *Transactions of the Institute of British Geographers, 38*(1), 65–77.

Ray. (2018). Rapid urban change demands a theory, tools and a 'fast forward' planning–an assay. In City planning in a Hyper dynamic Age, Ed. Perm, Russia: ISOCARP. Internet: https://isocarp.org/product/2012-48th-isocarp-congress-permrus.

Sanyal, R. (2014). Urbanizing refuge: Interrogating spaces of displacement. *International Journal of Urban and Regional Research, 38*(2), 558–572.

SBS. (2013). Syria Crisis. Retrieved from http://www.sbs.com.au/news/social-tags/syria-crisis.

Scavino, S. (2014). *The summerisation of Jordanian shelters*. Retrieved 04/2018, from https://issuu.com/scavinos/docs/the_summerization_stampa2.

Scullard, H. H., Salibi, Hamidé, K. S., Hourani, A.-R., Commins, A. H., Irvine, D. D., Smith, V. E., Ochsenwald, C. G., Polk, W. L., Roe, W., & Gadd, C. J. (2021). Syria. Encyclopedia Britannica. https://www.britannica.com/place/Syria.

Sigona, N. (2015). Campzenship: reimagining the camp as a social and political space. *Citizenship Studies, 19*(1), 1–15.

Smith, D. (2014). Somalia: Refugee camp brings solar energy into computer classrooms. Retrieved from https://womennewsnetwork.net/2013/08/12/somalia-refugee-camp-solar-computer.

Sphere Project. (2004). *Humanitarian charter and minimum standards in disaster response* (2nd ed.). Sphere.

SWP. (2020). *SWP research paper—swp-berlin.org*. Retrieved from https://www.swp-berlin.org/publications/products/research_papers/2020RP11_ReconstructionSyria.

Syrian refugee crisis: What you need to know and how to help—syrian arab republic. ReliefWeb. (2019). Retrieved from https://reliefweb.int/report/syrian-arab-republic/syrian-refugee-crisis-what-you-need-know-and-how-help.

Tozzi. (2009). *Progetto C.A.S.E.—L'AQUILA*. Retrieved 2020, from https://www.site.it/laquila-2009-progetto-c-a-s-e-un-modello-gia-pronto/.

Tran, M. (2013). Jordan's Zaatari Refugee Camp Mushrooms as Syrians Set Up Shop. The Guardian, Retrieved from: http://www.theguardian.com/global.

UNHCR, ExCom. (2004). 'Protracted refugee situations', Standing Committee, 30th Meeting, EC/54/SC/CRP.14, 10 June.

UNHCR. (2007a). *Handbook for emergencies*. United nations high commissioner for refugees.

UNHCR. (2007b). Conclusion on Children at Risk No. 107 (LVIII)—2007b. Retrieved December 05, 2020, from https://www.refworld.org/docid/471897232.html.

UNHCR Jordan: Zaatari Refugee Camp—factsheet, June 2021—jordan. ReliefWeb. (n.d.). Retrieved November 5, 2021, from https://reliefweb.int/report/jordan/unhcr-jordan-zaatari-refugee-camp-factsheet-june-2021?gclid=Cj0KCQjwqp-LBhDQARIsAO0a6aJJlF3lx1AkJ9IztjoovKoF-Nbikea1Mv-kYAelM1S1zBB-PAjf7X0aAlYbEALw_wcB.

UNHCR. (2012). Syria Regional Refugee Response (12 July 2012) (Amman: UNHCR).

UNHCR. (2013). UNHCR policy on alternatives to Camps. UNHCR Policy on Alternatives to Camps. Retrieved November 3, 2021, from https://cms.emergency.unhcr.org/documents/11982/45535/UNHCR+-+Policy+on+alternatives+to+camps/005c0217-7d1e-47c9-865a-c0098cfdda62.

UNHCR. (2014). Global strategy for settlement and shelter, A UNHCR Strategy 2014–2018 (1211 ed., Vol. 2). Geneva, Switzerland: United Nations High Commissioner for Refugees.

UNHCR. (2015). *Jordan's Zaatari refugee camp turns 3, challenges for the future of the thousands living there*. Retrieved 2020, from https://www.unhcr.org/news/briefing/2015/7/55b89a1a9/jordans-zaatari-refugee-camp-turns-3-challenges-future-thousands-living.html.

UNHCR. (2016). Dwelling modification in Za'atari camp. Retrieved from http://www.unhcr.org/innovation/labs_post/dwelling-modification-zaatari-camp.

UNHCR. (2017). UNHCR Syria Regional Refugee Response. Retrieved from http://data.unhcr.org/syrianrefugees/regional.php.

UNHCR. (2019). Refugee statistics. UNHCR. Retrieved from https://www.unhcr.org/refugee-statistics/.

UNHCR. (2020a). *United Nations Office on Genocide prevention and the responsibility to protect*. Retrieved March 23, 2020a, from https://www.un.org/en/genocideprevention/.

UNHCR. (2020b). *Voluntary Returns of Syrian Refugees: Regional analysis*. Retrieved 2020b, from https://data2.unhcr.org/en/.

UNHCR. (2020c). Zaatari Refugee Camp—Factsheet, July 2020c—Jordan. Retrieved, 2020c, from https://reliefweb.int/report/jordan/zaatari-refugee-camp-factsheet-july-2020.

UNHCR. (2020d). Zaatari Refugee Camp—Factsheet, July 2020d—Jordan. Retrieved December 06, 2020d, from https://reliefweb.int/report/jordan/zaatari-refugee-camp-factsheet-july-2020.

UNHCR. (2021). Zaatari Refugee Camp—Factsheet, January 2021—Jordan. Retrieved, 2021, from https://reliefweb.int/report/jordan/zaatari-refugee-camp-factsheet-January-2021.

UNHCR. (2022). Donate to help Syrian refugees who have fled war and violence. UNHCR. Retrieved from https://donate.unhcr.org/int/en/syria-emergency?gclid=EAIaIQobChMI0LPO86ih9QIVWoKDBx1bUAF-EAAYAiAAEgKG4PD_BwE&gclsrc=aw.ds.

UNOSAT. (2009). Dadaab refugee camps-overview-garissa, N. Eastern, Kenya (as of 04 Jul 2009)-kenya. ReliefWeb. Retrieved from https://reliefweb.int/map/kenya/dadaab-refugee-camps-overview-garissa-n-eastern-kenya-04-jul-2009.

UNRWA. (2017). Baqa'a Camp. UNRWA. Retrieved from https://www.unrwa.org/where-we-work/jordan/baqaa-camp.

UNRWA. (2019a). *Amman new camp*. Retrieved from https://www.unrwa.org/where-we-work/jordan/amman-new-camp.

UNRWA. (2019b). *Palestine refugees in Jordan*. Retrieved 2020, from https://www.unrwa.org/palestine-refugees.

UNRWA. (2020). Palestine Refugees. UNRWA. Retrieved from https://www.unrwa.org/palestine-refugees#:~:text=A%20Palestine%20refugee%20camp%20is,are%20not%20recognized%20as%20camps.

URBACT. (2021). Thessaloniki. URBACT. Retrieved from https://urbact.eu/thessaloniki.

Vaughan, L. (1997). The urban 'GHETTO' the spatial distribution of ethnic minorities. *Urban Themes, 2*, 241–2414.

Wind, B., & Ibrahim, B. (2020, January 14). The war-time urban development of Damascus: How the geography- and political economy of warfare affects housing patterns. Retrieved October 04, 2020, from https://www.sciencedirect.com/science/article/pii/S0197397519309464.

Woroniecka–Krzyzanowska, D. (2017). The right to the camp: Spatial politics of protracted 195 encampment in the West Bank. *Political Geography, 61* (November), 160–9.

Zampano, G., Moloney, L., & Juan, J. (2015). Migrant crisis: A history of displacement. *The Wall Street Journal*. Retrieved from http://graphics.wsj.com/migrant-crisis-a-history-of-displacement.

Chapter 2
The Urbicide

Abstract Violence toward a city could be direct or indirect. This chapter argues the politics of urban destruction in cities, presenting two types of urbicide: the direct urbicide and the indirect urbicide to develop an integrated approach to planning in emergencies by understanding the integrated planning process and analyzing its opportunities and limits in the temporary settlements. Integrated planning promotes an adaptable mechanism that is socially responsible for improving the citizens' life quality however this study reveals the insufficiency in the integrated planning approach to be applied as it is in the post-conflict resettlement issue. Because it lacks what so-called "space-time" approach, which stands on a quick response to urgent needs with long-term solutions. Consequently, shifting the current policies in dealing with such urban phenomena from short-term practices to a permanent and sustainable approach. To be target-oriented and implementation-oriented within a specific timeframe that is committed to serving the refugee community's needs and aspirations with equal opportunities to create an integrated community within the integrated built environment to face the challenges of refuge and post-conflict situations.

Keywords Urbicide · Direct urbicide · Indirect urbicide · Integrated spatial planning

2.1 The Concept of Urbicide

The urban process of any city is a ceaseless process of "rise and fall," of destruction and construction, of a continuous transformation, modification, and development (Kostof & Tobias, 1999). The city's urban tissue, with its components, is susceptible to different natural and human-made hazards that partially or wholly impact its identity.

This chapter argues the politics of urban destruction in cities. In other words, *"urbicide,"* the term consisted of two words that refer to Latin origins: *urbs,* which means "city" and *occido,* which literally means "to massacre." In plain English, "the violence against the city." It is the destruction of a city and its character; it is a kind of violence that targets the city's urban tissue (Urban dictionary, 2020). The first documented adoption for this term went back to the English author Michael Moorcock in 1963 in the Elric novella "Dead God's Homecoming" (Moorcock, 1963). Gradually, the term urbicide starts being used increasingly in the late sixties by architects—such as a group of Bosnian architects in 1992 in their work "Mostar 92"—urban planners and urban critics—such as Ada Louis Huxtable in 1972, Bogdan Bogdanović in 1987, and Marshall Berman in 1996—to interpret and to comprehend the impact of wars on the city's urban fabric. The term urbicide consists of two interwoven concepts: the city and the violence. Henry Lefebvre (2016) has defined the city, "A city is, therefore, whether it is experienced, known, represented, constructed, or destroyed as a city." The concept of a city is clear enough to be recognized but hard to be defined with fixed features; it is a combination of tangible and intangible elements that shape its form and identity. From one side, it is a collective of systems—economic, political, and health; furthermore, it is an accumulation of social and cultural norms, behaviors, and manners. On the other side, it is a conglomeration of solid (masses) and voids (open spaces) in addition to its infrastructure. As the urban historian Lewis Mumford (1961) stated: "Perhaps the best definition of the city in its higher aspects is to say that it is a place designed to offer the widest facilities for significant conversation."

Consequently, violence toward the city impacts both its physical, tangible parts, and the intangible features.

For this reason, some scholars claimed that urbicide should be linked and studied as part of genocide which was defined by the United Nations Genocide Convention as "acts committed with intent to destroy, in whole or in part, a national, ethnic, racial or religious group, as such" (United Nations [UN], 2020). Because in the way you destroy the people's homes, you sabotage them. Urbicide term is a concept with a hybrid nature that implies understanding it either as a comprehensive framework to observe and analyze the historical destruction of cities or as something "exclusive" appropriate only to the "current moment" and has instantly necessary qualities. Specific zones in the city shape a form of pirate urbanism and generate a kind of violence toward the city (Granham, 2007).

For instance, what could be seen in slums and refugee camps where the physical destruction is not visible but because of the undesirable living conditions. Consequently, war victims in these temporary zones are suffering from the quality and quantity of essential services with a lack of accessibility to public amenities, and as we called it in this book "indirect urbicide." The indirect urbicide causes unintentional yet excessive, and irremediable harm to the city urban fabric and its inhabitants because of the use of the inappropriate feeble planning strategies. As a result, cities face high risks because of decrepit housing conditions, deteriorated and insufficient infrastructure, molding new informalities over the hosting countries' urban fabric.

For example, two types of urbicide created by the Syrian civil war can be classified: First, the direct urbicide which refers to the violence toward the Syrian cities and the devastation caused by the war. Second, the indirect urbicide, which refers to the refugee camp's problems in cities that host the Syrian refugees.

2.2 Direct Urbicide in Syrian Cities

Violence against cities is not something new. It has its deep roots in history, and such events continue to arise from time to time. As has been discussed by Marshall Berman (2018), an American Marxist writer and political theorist, that urbicide is the oldest story in the world. Amidst long records, for example, the destruction of Jerusalem by the Roman Empire and a similarly devastating Carthaginian peace, the destruction of Tenochtitlan, Moscow, Dresden and Tokyo, and the use of the nuclear weapon by US military against Hiroshima and Nagasaki in 1945 (Etaywe, 2017), the Nazis' destruction of Warsaw after the 1944 Warsaw Uprising, as well as the Siege of Sarajevo, the prolonged Israeli–Palestinian conflict, destruction of Zimbabwe which is associated with the Bosnian Wars of the early 1990s, post-Katrina New Orleans in August 2005, and the American invasion of Iraq in 2003. On March 15, 2011, Syria witnessed the breakout after the Arab Spring sparked in Tunisia and Egypt and forced out the presidents of Tunisia and Egypt in 2010 (Aljazeera, 2017). What became known as the Arab Spring reached Syria and rapidly turned to an aggressive political revolution and an aggressive civil war (Aljazeera, 2017). The Syrian cities' status after the Syrian civil war has become an absolute catastrophe. The architectural masterpieces and built heritages dating back centuries have been extirpated, crowded marketplaces turned ghostly empty, and basic infrastructure has been smashed into dust, they have transformed completely into scenes of apocalyptic devastation (McKenzie, 2018). The conflict has now (as of 2021) entered its tenth year since March 15th, 2011, having killed hundreds of thousands of people and forced about half of the pre-war population to flee internally or cross-borders (World Vision, 2020). This civil war in Syria has caused more than 5.6 million Syrian to flee their country, and 6.2 million are internally displaced (UNHCR, 2020). Syria exposed to multisided armed groups that magnified the damaging effect of this catastrophe. This armed conflict has killed more than half a million Syrian and has destroyed Syria's infrastructure, heritage sites, worship places, healthcare facilities, and housing (Akkoc, 2016). For example, according to the World Health Organization (WHO) 50% of hospitals in Syria have been damaged and destroyed (Akkoc, 2016). Moreover, in the first two years of the war, 3900 schools have been completely or partially damaged or subjugated by conflict parties for non-educational purposes (The Guardian, 2013). Aljazeera (2015) reported that more than 290 cultural and heritage sites had been affected where 104 of them were damaged, 24 of them destroyed, and 83% of UNESCO World Heritage sites in the country were damaged. During the war in Syria, the assaults on, and destruction of Palmyra resembled the destruction of the world-historical monuments elsewhere—as of the Stari Most in the city of Mostar in Bosnia and Herzegovina (Azzouz, 2019). The siege and destruction of the Stari Most became a representative event of urbicide in the 1992–95 Bosnian War. The ottoman bridge Mostar's Stari manifests the local pride and the co-existence of diverse religious and ethnic groups (Grodach, 2002). The assault on and destruction of the bridge became stereotypical of the more massive violence that was consuming the former Yugoslav republic of Bosnia–Herzegovina (Coward, 2009). By the same token, Palmyra became a memorial for cultural loss and the destruction of identity for both state and population (Doppelhofer, 2016). Historically, Syria is considered an important habitat of ancient civilizations through history. In essence, several civilizations have settled in Syria such as Acheulian, Mustrian, Neolithic, Halaf, Sumerian, Acadian, Babylonian, Assyrian, Hittite, Aramaic, Hellenistic, Roman, Byzantine, Islamic, and Ottoman (Akkermans & Schwartz, 2003). Syrian cultural heritage sites are distributed in three major areas: Mesopotamia area, Northwest Syria, and South Syria (Kanjou, 2018). However, the brutal violence in Syria and a lack of security have destroyed several heritage sites and archeological museums (Kanjou, 2018). As discussed by Mahfouz (2021), the destruction of Aleppo has disrupted Aleppo's cultural and social practices of its historical part.

The heritage damage in Syria has occurred through three destructive practices; first, due to military conflict including airplanes strikes, bombs, and shoots alongside with the damage that was caused by the occupation of other conflict groups to some historical sites and deliberately sabotaged them (Kanjou, 2018). For instance, the destruction of Aleppo historical center in the old city of Aleppo after the Battle of Aleppo (2012–2016) (Affaki, 2021). The conflict in Aleppo has severely impacted the old Aleppo city, Aleppo castle, Umayyad Mosque, Aleppo National museum, old market, and commercial market. Moreover, Homes, Aleppo, and Deir Ez Zor are occupied by ISIS and other militias groups (Kanjou, 2018). Second, illegal excavation: the absence of protection in non-government and anti-government regions has increased the threat of illegal excavation, especially in the most important heritage sites (Kanjou, 2018). Unknown armed groups excavated and stole precious discoveries in Dead city and Apamea in the Hellenistic Roman–Byzantine period (Kanjou, 2018). Third, Robbery: Syrian archaeological museums suffered from robbing of more than 4000 pieces of antiques as well as other stolen and hidden relics (Kanjou, 2018).

The armed conflict in Syria has mainly targeted educational institutions, healthcare facilities, housing, roads, power supplies, and sewage system. Although attacking hospital and safety zones is considered an illegal act according to the First and Fourth Geneva convention, Syrian hospital suffered from airstrikes and blasting of its facilities (Karasapan, 2015). The ongoing conflict in Syria negatively impacted the healthcare system in Syria by the direct attack to follow the fleeing people and combatants (Karasapan, 2015). Those military operations destroyed 50% of hospitals in Syria. Besides, ISIS exploded more than 12 healthcare centers in 2015 (Karasapan, 2015). The education system in Syria has not been so far from violence. Still, it has been negatively impacted by civil war, as more than one in three schools are either damaged, destroyed or no longer in use for educational purposes (Humanitarian Need Overview [HNO], 2019). There is more than a million of Syrian children are not attending schools, and there is a notable deterioration of education quality and contradiction in curricula content. This matter was further aggravated due to the threat of armed attacks on schools and controlling of other groups on schools which has increased the vulnerabilities of educational facilities and infrastructure (Zyck, 2011). The World Bank (2014) estimated the damage of the education sector in major six Syrian cities (not including rebuilding cost) was 248 million for 2014. Since Assad's troops and their ally attacked residential areas in Syria, and they used chemical and missile weapons against civilians leaving behind the dead, victims, and destruction in urban areas (Goldman, 2015). In 2016, Assad's troops completely devastated Aleppo city and refuged its remaining people (Goldman, 2015). The violence in Syria targeted population centers and people's homes, which makes the ruins and destruction everywhere (Goldman, 2015) that requires a rigorous response to the housing and shelter need to enable Syrians to recover from their homes' loss as a repercussion of this civil war.

Remarkably, the legacy of violence and destruction is indisputable across the country. The suffering of the Syrian civilians continues growing with the absence of the necessary conditions for a proper life because homes, schools, hospitals, and other primary facilities have been damaged and destroyed, the large-scale destruction in urban contexts has created a vast number of cross-sector challenges. The damage to infrastructure is a critical issue that impacts all elements of life (REACH, 2019). What happened in Syria resembled the destruction of Afghanistan, as Larry Goodson (2001, p. 94) notes " at one point or another … virtually everything in Afghanistan has been a target. Cities, towns, villages, houses, mosques and minarets, schools, hospitals, industrial structures, other buildings, roads, bridges, orchards, and fields have all been damaged or destroyed during combat." It should be noted that "rubbleisation" is different from a scorched earth strategy. Insofar a scorched earth strategy aims to destroy the built environment, the infrastructure, or anything that might be useful to the enemy, such as weapons, transport vehicles, communication sites, and technical resources. While Rubbleisation, as its name suggests, is intended to reduce the built environment to rubble (Coward, 2009). Rubbleisation is the scenario that happened and is still happening in Syria's case, which is considered one of the most brutal urban conflicts in recent years (The International Institute for Strategic Studies [IISS], 2017). During the Syrian civil war, 53% of the Syrian population living in urban areas were hit by weighty aerial strikes and fighting within towns and cities (World Bank, 2017). The impact of those severe bombardments is observable in civilians' daily life who get used to living within a totally, moderately, or partially damaged built environment, as illustrated in Fig. 2.1. To put in evidence, as the Informing More Effective Humanitarian Action "REACH" (2019) reported on the infrastructure damage of 16 towns and cities across Syria, classifying their buildings based on satellite-detected damage analysis into destroyed, severely damaged, or moderately damaged. The buildings' damage categorization was according to UNITAR-UNOSAT (2015) model that considered a building as (1) destroyed building; when between 75 and 100% of the building structure is destroyed, in other words, all or most parts of the structure are collapsed; (2) severely damaged buildings, when between 30 and 75% of the structure is destroyed, that is a significant part of the building structure collapsed; (3) moderately damaged buildings, when between 5 and 30% of the structure is damaged, that's to say, the building structure demonstrates limited damage. See Fig. 2.2 for the number of damaged or destroyed buildings in Syria.

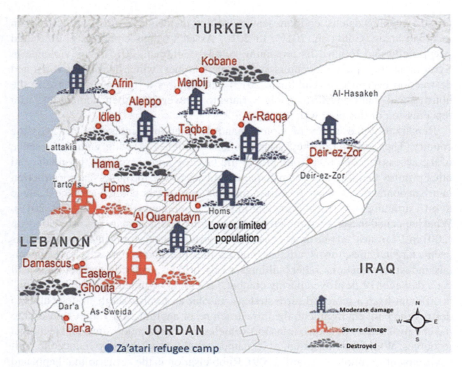

Fig. 2.1 Damage assessment distribution map. Ref: By the author 2020. Data retrieved from REACH, (2019)

2.3 Indirect Urbicide, "Conflict-Induced Displacement and the Right to the City"

When conflict drags on for a long time as it is in the case of the Syrian civil war, it transforms people's life into misery. They awaited in an agony of suspension, and then they will find themselves forced to flee seeking safety, security, and better living conditions. The distinctive feature of the direct urbicide is the deliberate destruction of the built environment that occurs as a result of areal strikes and bombardments, as evidenced in the iconic event of destroying the Stari Most that put the destruction of the built environment into the political agenda (Coward, 2009). Antagonistically, the new phenomenon introduced by this study as indirect urbicide is the "the refugee camps," which connected to the invisible violence toward the city, by way of explanation, when the physical destruction of the buildings is not visible. Still, it appears in the construction process and short-term planning strategies of the temporary settlement in emergencies where the basic requirements are in short supply and over time. They generate profound modifications to the city's territorial structure, they shape a new identity, and they create a contentious change in the city's form and history.

2.3 Indirect Urbicide, "Conflict-Induced Displacement …

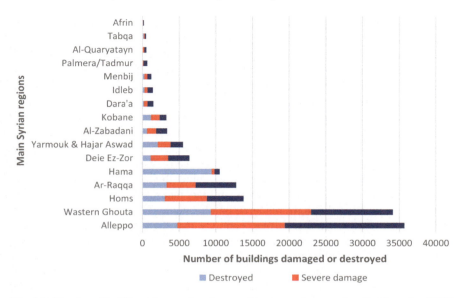

Fig. 2.2 Number of buildings damaged or destroyed by town, city or region. By the author 2020| Data retrieved from REACH, (2019)

Fig. 2.3 Ain Helweh camp in Lebanon. Ref: Dettmer, 2013

See Fig. 2.3 how the Ain Hilweh refugee camp for the Palestinian refugees near the port of Sidon city in Lebanon has been transformed into a slum-like neighborhood.

Consequently, the destruction targeting the built environments is not confined to situations of inter-state conflict but also linked to other human actions capable of shredding the built environment. Indeed, urban theorists such as Ada Louise Huxtable (1972) and Marshal Berman (1996) discussed that some projects, even in normal situations, unveil "administrative" destruction. They argued that the development of New York City was responsible for the bureaucratic damage of substantial sections of the built environment to clear space for projects such as Robert Moses' Cross Bronx Expressway or the World Trade Center. Mike Davis (2002) lists similar kinds of destruction in his book the Dead Cities. He examines themes of the urban life in areas he calls national sacrifice zones, which are military landscapes that simulated warfare and arms production that have rendered uninhabitable. Porteous and Smith (2001) pursue this theme somewhat further, claiming that the contemporary era testifies to the "global destruction of home" through administrative projects such as dam building. By the same token, Taraki (2011) argued that urbicide could be achieved not only by destruction but also through construction and control. Indeed, the negative consequence of lousy reconstruction is highly noticed in the case of refugee camps, this poses the urgent need to raise the indirect urbicide onto the urban and political agenda.

Forced displacement, especially in protracted crises, has dramatically increased unavoidable adverse risks, which significantly affect humans' well-being and a city's urban structure. The arising conflicts worldwide increased not only the number of refugees but the number and size of refugee camps (United Nations High Commissioner for Refugees [UNHCR], 2018). Jordan is a case exemplifies how refugee camps stand for decades and are being transformed into fragile cities. At the same time, there is a notable increase in the body of literature that discusses the challenge of providing a good quality of life for vast numbers of people congesting in our cities today (The Royal Institution of Chartered Surveyors [RICS], 2018). Comfort, well-being, and quality of life concepts are considered important objectives in different contexts such as justice, economy, or the environment (Fracolli et al., 2011), as well as urban planning and design. The adoption of indicators of material, social, and psychological needs satisfaction has become a vital tool in assessing the quality of life and identifying and evaluating comfort and well-being characteristics (Mishchuk & Grishnova, 2015). Quality of life is considered a critical aspect in sustaining any urban environment (Serag El-Din et al., 2012), and the planner aims to upgrade comfort and well-being in every setting and for all inhabitants (Lotfi & Solaimani, 2009). The quality of life in cities cannot be enhanced by depending only on brick and mortar. It requires personal satisfaction with different urban and social attributes such as population and building densities, service availability, accessibility of essential goods, quality of public spaces, protecting public health, and providing safety, security, and education (Serag El-Din et al., 2012). Refugees' and migrants' comfort, well-being, and quality of life have been extensively examined in different fields such as political science, health care, education, built environment, and international development. Refugee camps should be studied with an urban logic considering them emerging urban environments with a population equivalent to regular cities (De Rooij et al., 2016). Like any unplanned metropolitan area suffering from social, political, environmental, and economic problems, they are just like any unplanned metropolitan area, and there is an obvious need to understand their failure in providing comfort, well-being, and good quality of life.

Consequently, the idea of indirect urbicide in refugee camps is concerned with the impact of the prolonged existence of the camp settlements over the urban tissue and their transformation into deteriorated spaces. Because refugee camps become nodes of unplanned zoned without any historical, cultural, organizational connection with the city urban fabric, ignoring particularly its spatial and socio-cultural dimensions. The spatial configuration of these zones resembles the politics of exclusion, "anti-heterogeneity" (Coward, 2002).

2.4 Post-conflict Urban Reconstruction and Redefining a Place to Live In

Reconstruction is generally considered as an approach that innovatively resolves development issues (Brun & Lund, 2008). While PCR process has been described by Theron (2011) as the process of rebuilding the country and achieving sustainable peace, in the context of security, political governance, socio-economic development, gender, and justice which effectively engage and empower the local communities and through this, we approach the real recovery. A successful reconstruction in post-conflict situations requires a deep understanding of the political environment, effective coordination between a wide range of local community stakeholders. Besides, implementing active consultation among the collaborators, which is a crucial factor in the process of finding out the essential and most needed components of the planning systems and processes (Earnest, 2015). However, there is a notable disparagement of the employed methods of reconstruction in post-conflict situations, which is prominently lacking an appropriate exit strategy that able to cover issues of funding, resources, and planning (O'Driscoll, 2018).

As argued by Earnest (2015), the international implementing agencies which get involved during emergencies, such as the UN organizations, come to the emergency field carrying their package of organizational, operational, and executive policies, rather than developing them in the context. This approach is the crux of the problem; the rigidity in working with emergency is not suitable anymore but instead worsens it especially in historic cities. As Arefian (2020) discussed, the presence of a historical layer in cities adds more complexities to the post-disaster reconstruction process because it requires the involvement of disaster management, urban development, and heritage maintenance systems together.

Creating resilience requires strong roots that anchored the policy to the ground of context "context-specified" approach, but it needs flexible branches to adapt to unpredictable conditions. According to O'Driscoll (2018), reconstruction decisions should surpass the traditional conception of the term "with a focus on physical rebuilding or the reconstruction of political institutions and public services" and should also consider the societal repair.

It is necessary to create high levels of integration and cooperation between the decision-makers both in public and the private spheres also engaging the local community (Arefian, 2018).

As the nature of post-conflict context is a set of changing dynamics; for that reason, humanitarian agencies and other concerned agencies should demonstrate high levels of flexibility during the planning and executive phases. This approach means a full and active engagement of the local members in all aspects of the reconstruction project from the decision-making to the implementation (Earnest, 2015), as confirmed by Saul (2014) that the local community engagement in the decision-making phase is decisive for establishing efficient reconstruction projects. The reason behind empowering the local population, according to Saul (2014), the stricken population has a sharp and translucent view for the situation, and they are conscious of their needs. In that way, the reconstruction act will have a broader perspective to include more competent components that will create a more comprehensive and integrated project. Francis (2016) argued that the current planning policies in post-conflict reconstruction employ short-term solutions and seek a quick fix by formulating bare policies as an exit strategy within the near future. For instance, the short-term policies implemented by the international community concerning the post-conflict reconstruction in South Sudan express their failures and insufficiency such as missing common ground for a participatory government and the lacking support from local and international communities (Annan, 2019). Also, the absence of concrete, tangible reconstruction measures capable of providing both safety and satisfaction for populations in immediate need of a welfare system. Constructing projects aiming at a quick exit rather than focusing on social development (Pugh, 1998).

Different frameworks have been created to deal with post-conflict reconstruction within a specific focus. For instance, The Center for Strategic and International Studies (CSIS) and the Association of the United States Army (AUSA) (2002) generated a reconstruction framework that requires security through incorporating all aspects of collective and individual public safety). Security considered as a precondition for effective reconstruction outcomes besides justice, reconciliation, social and economic well-being, governance, and participation. While the United Nations Human Settlements Programme (UN-Habitat) (2017) argued that a successful reconstruction process claims government support and the engagement of the local community. However, The African Post-Conflict Reconstruction Policy Framework developed by the New Partnership for Africa's Development (NEPAD) requires involving a diverse wide range of actors. They recommended engaging Economic Community (RECs), Member State, civil society, financial and private sector in Africa, international institutions, agencies, government, NGOs, and private contractors (NEPAD, 2005) for a successful reconstruction process. Sakalasuriya et al., (2017) established a conceptual framework as a comprehensive reference to analyze the consequences of post-conflict reconstruction (PCR) within four main categories: economic, social, political, and environmental repercussions, connecting them with the context, intervention, and long-term outcomes.

Indeed, the post-conflict reconstruction and the visible impacts of the repatriation process for the Syrians may be the tip of the iceberg, specifically regarding the housing issue, either by having access to their properties "Housing Land Properties [HLP]" or the urgent need for a fully functional city. The repatriation of the Syrian refugees is the process of their return to their place of origin. Either as refugees, internally displaced, or sometimes a second-generation immigrant to their ancestors' land, or over-stayers, a rejected asylum seeker, or those who are unwilling to stay more in the established refugee camps in Jordan, Lebanon, Turkey, and other countries.

The brutal conflict in Syria is not only confined to those hundreds of thousands who were killed, or to that nation which has been torn into parts, or that living standards that sit back for decades but the deliberate destruction which targeted people's homes. Hundreds of thousands Syrians have lost their homes or have been forcibly displaced from them (Azzouz, 2019). They are not only suffering from losing their property, but also their safety, dignity, identity, self-esteem, and their social relationships because the destruction of a home is "a powerful symbolic erosion of security, social well-being, and place attachment" (Boano and Astolfo, 2011, P.38). Despite the difficult conditions in Syria, the Syrian refugees voluntarily return to their homes. As shown in Fig. 2.4 that UNHCR (2018) has registered 1.4 million voluntary Syrian refugee returns. Despite the ongoing conflict, besides the very challenging conditions in Syria, UNHCR anticipated around 234,817 refugee returns in 2020.

In summary, Post-conflict reconstruction (PCR) is a multifaceted process that combines simultaneous short-, medium- and long-term programs as in Fig. 2.5 which demonstrates the linkages between PCR interventions and their consequences. It involves different actors in the whole reconstruction process from the emergency, the

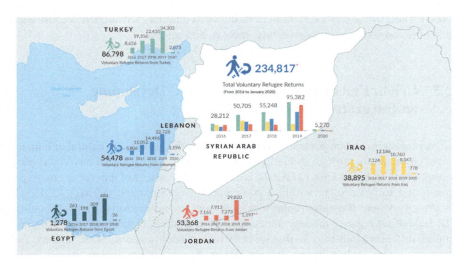

Fig. 2.4 The voluntary Syrian refugee returns. Ref: UNHCR (2020)

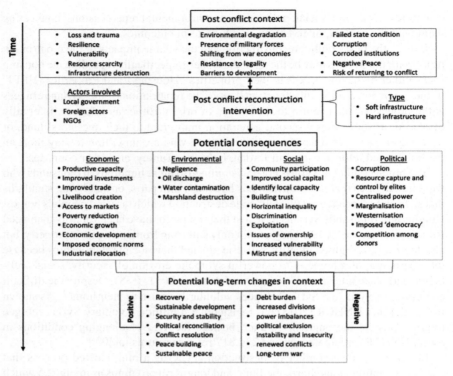

Fig. 2.5 PCR-Conceptual framework of Sakalasuriya, Haigha & Amaratunga (2017)

transition, and the development phase, aiming at building sustainable peace (NEPAD, 2005). Therefore, every PCR framework has been uniquely formulated because each one relies on its specific components, context, and actors.

2.5 Urban Emergency Management and Developing an Integrated Approach to Planning

Urban emergency management could be defined as the response to natural or human-induced incidents through the field of city planning, to react with any emergency event within an urban lens, to take the concepts and practices of emergency management, and to place them within a contemporary environment (Henkey, 2018). It is the city where the catastrophe hits, and from it, the recovery starts. In reality, the field of emergency management concerns in dealing, controlling, and administrating different kinds of risks that severely impact communities, cities, regions, and sometimes the whole country, assigning them in a state of emergency.

The main aim of emergency management is to minimize or avoid potential losses from risks, to provide immediate and proper assistance to damaged materials, and to achieve speedy and effective recovery through the five phases of disaster management: prevention, preparedness, mitigation, response, and recovery (CCAHA, 2019). Prevention aims to avoid human hazards by outlining excessive permanent protection measures from disasters. Nevertheless, not all accidents can be prevented. But with reliable evacuation plans, proper environmental planning, and design standards, the jeopardy could be controlled (Bexar, 2020). Then the mitigation phase includes a series of actions taken to prevent or reduce the cause, impact, and consequences of disasters, and it implements structural and non-structural measures to reduce the effects of risks (FEMA, 2004). The preparedness phase requires developing educational sessions, training programs, and planning activities; it focuses on the exercising measures to increase the readiness in responding to all emergencies (Bexar, 2020). The response phase happens in the immediate aftermath of a disaster, while life doesn't function normally (FEMA, 2004). It requires successful coordination and rational resources management (Bexar, 2020). The last phase on the cycle is the recovery phase, which begins directly after subsiding the threat to human life, aiming at regaining the normal functionality of life (CCAHA, 2019).

"Urban Emergency Management: Planning and Response for the 21st Century" by Thomas Henkey (2017) guides both natural and human-induced hazards across all phases of emergency management: prevention, preparedness, mitigation, response, and recovery in which Henkey calls the attention of planners to the issue of emergency management in urban areas which has not yet been fully explored (McArthur, 2018). Indeed, the main goal of spatial planning is to achieve territorial sustainability (Camagni, 2017) and it is a technical and sociopolitical process that aims to develop the built environment, enhance the public welfare, organize the land uses, and protect the natural environment (Taylor, 1998). The urban planning field guides the development through different scopes, such as economic, sociopolitical, and public health. They cover various scales, including urban and regional planning, town and city planning, rural and sub-urban development (Caves, 2004) by engaging professionals from different fields in engineering, social sciences, and design sciences, who for a long time worked independently. This approach created cities with chronic urban dilemmas, such as social injustice, unemployment, traffic congestion, and environmental pollution (Milojevic, 2018). Cities continuously suffer from these problems, and this leads to "the importance of across space-and-time planning approaches. An approach that accounts for short- and long-term consequences and multiple levels of impacts of city and metropolitan-scale problems, including local, regional, and national levels" (Abukhater, 2009. p.67) and as a result, unsustainable nature of urban form has occurred (Visser, 2001).

The global response to the current urban phenomena such as the refugee crisis, climate change, epidemics, and economic recession, expresses the need for an integrated approach to urban planning. These phenomena require serious sustainable development strategies and permanent, sustainable planning models to create resilient environments. Integrated Spatial Planning or ISP refers to the contemporary urban development strategies and approaches aiming at achieving maximum sustainable utilization of the context, including the placement of people, facilities, and infrastructure maintaining the territorial quality, efficiency, and identity (Camagni, 2017).

The United Nations institutions have outlined different spatial planning implications, such as the New Urban Agenda (UN-Habitat, 2020), which reveal an attitude in integrated planning by creating a new correspondence between efficient urbanization and development. Besides stressing the relationship between proper urbanization and job creation, livelihood opportunities, and upgraded life quality, which should be covered in any urban renewal policy and strategy (The New Urban Agenda [NUA], 2017). The target is to create a balanced correlation between short-term needs and the long-term desired outcomes of a competitive economy, high quality of life, and a sustainable environment (Milojevic, 2018). The Agenda encompasses different strategic implications of planning and management of urban and spatial development through balanced policies for territorial expansion, participatory approach, developing more public spaces, enhancing the quality of buildings, promoting the multiple uses of space. The New Urban Agenda corresponds with the 2030 Agenda for sustainable development, particularly the Goal 11—"make cities and human settlements inclusive, resilient, and sustainable" (The United Nations UN], 2015, P.14). Making cities sustainable means "creating career and business opportunities, safe and affordable housing, and building resilient societies and economies. It involves investment in public transport, creating green public spaces, and improving urban planning and management in participatory and inclusive ways" (The United Nations Development Program [UNDP], 2020).

2.5.1 *The Methodology Process of an Integrated Planning*

The integrated nature of the urban phenomenon and the planning process has guided the development of the theories of integrated planning (Milojevic, 2018). To develop a methodology of the integrated planning process, planning theorists found it necessary to move from the traditional land use planning to strategic planning, which focuses on integrated development through its process, guidelines, and institutional design. To shift from the materialistic solution to social problems in traditional planning to strategic plans that work through short-term steps, and to outline the activities of stakeholders to discuss the reasons for the spatial changes and to propose appropriate solutions (Milojevic, 2018). The concept of integrated planning has been defined by Albrecht (2004) as a four-track approach with conditional integration of different models of rationality: value rationality that aims at designing alternative futures; communicative rationality which involves a growing number of actors in the process; instrumental rationality that seeks the best way, and the most highly techniques to solve current problems and achieve the aspired future; and strategic rationality through a clear and precise strategy for dealing with power relationships.

2.5 Urban Emergency Management and Developing …

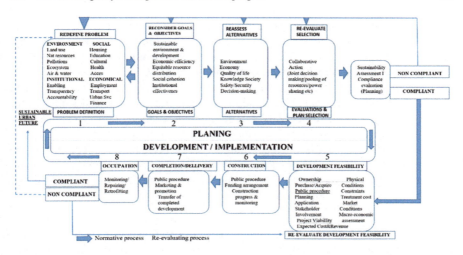

Fig. 2.6 Proposed integrated urban planning and development process. Ref Teriman (2012)

Adopting a systems approach involves the integration of the three key components—planning, development, and ecosystem sustainability—into a single urban planning and development process to create a sustainability-oriented urban planning and development culture (Yigitcanlar & Teriman, 2014, p. 346). In this approach, the role of urban planners has been revised to be more active in moderating and communicating with the stakeholders rather than being exclusively restricted to provide expert evaluation and technical leadership (ibid). Teriman (2012) has developed a model for integrated planning approach which entails eight steps: (1) redefine the problems in the domains of environment, society, economy, and institutions; (2) reconsider goals and objectives; (3) reassess alternatives; (4) re-evaluate selection; (5) development feasibility; (6) construction; (7) completion/delivery; and (8) occupation. As illustrated in Fig. 2.6

Integrated planning requires a set of technical and tactical acts to create sustainable urban developments concerning different measures and dimensions of sustainability. From a technical perspective, it is necessary to: firstly: develop a multidisciplinary analysis for all the environmental factors that impact the planning process, such as geomorphology, geology, seismology, natural resources, renewable energy resources, vegetation, climate, and climate change. In addition to various factors generated by human activities like the construction of urban facilities or the urban destruction after conflicts and wars on residential housing, educational institutions, social/health facilities, and the economy. It requires detailed damage assessment reports that help redefine the problems, goals, and objectives of planning regarding the complexity of the urban context. Secondly, relinquishing the strict regulatory planning and obtaining the flexibility of integrated planning by using zoning (Counsell & Allmendinger, 2006) because it offers versatility in defining building roles, parcels of land, and permitted, conditionally permitted, and prohibited land use. Consequently, a dynamic social, economic, and environmental urban context (Kosareva & Puzanov, 2012) can be more easily acquired in the planning process. GIS technology has been considered a useful tool to formulate a database for sustainable planning and management of different spatial scales and resources (Rotondo & Selocato, 2014).

From the strategic "tactic" perspective, the integrated approach looks to the city in means of time and space. Consequently, the integrated character focuses on the best way to regulate all "timescales" (short, medium, and long term) and all "spatial scales" [regional/metropolitan area/ small, medium, large size cities and towns and neighborhoods, etc.] and the concomitant between both of them. The process of integrated urban planning in creating urban development is flexible to the dynamics of change, engaging local stakeholders, and benefiting the local resources for best measurable results (UNDP, 2013). It should be:

- **Strategic** in shaping a flexible project vision and objectives on short, medium, and long terms, in determining a comprehensive orientation toward implementation, and in focusing on the participation of the local actors and citizens in the planning and decision-making process.
- **Sustainable** by protecting the environment and engaging the local community effectively.
- **Comprehensive** by adjusting the spatial, economic, social, and environmental components to be more integrated.
- **Participative** by involving all relevant stakeholders in a structured manner and by investing productively in all the available resources.
- **Operational** by regulating the arrangement of the actions within a specific timeframe.
- **Financial resources** by proposing suitable plans and policies of financial support.

2.6 Conclusion

As cities are at the first line of defense during conflicts and they are the key actors in development, besides, they are the real crucial need for every human being. Consequently, even the one who flees seeking safety and security far from conflict or that one who returns to his own home after the dispute is resolved needs a fully functional city. The need for a permanent, sustainable, and well-planned city requires the development of a new informal planning approach. Due to the fact that there is no such thing as stand-alone planning theory because planning is a discipline that concerns human life which is by its nature intensely complex and mixes different entries and relies on adopting ideas and principles from other practices (Allmendinger, 2002). Remarkably, there is an insufficiency in the integrated planning approach to be applied as it is in the post-conflict resettlement issue in terms of what so-called "space-time" planning approach in which stands on a quick response to urgent needs with long-term solutions. Consequently, shifting the current policies in dealing with such urban phenomena from short-term practices to a permanent and sustainable approach. To be target-oriented and implementation-oriented within a specific timeframe that committed to serving the refugee community needs and aspirations with equal opportunities for the sake of creating an integrated community within the integrated built environment to face the challenges of refuge and post-conflict situations.

The lack of a multiscale planning framework culminates in various critical problems that continue to appear while planning in and after emergency events. The integrated approach to planning is partial and selective, although different aspirations to make it comprehensive and holistic (Tornberg, 2011) as Macrori and Marvin (2019) argued that integration in practice is contradicted with the integration, in theory, revealing on partial and selective methods.

References

Abukhater. (2009). Rethinking planning theory and practice: A glimmer of light for prospects of integrated planning to combat complex urban realities. *Theoretical and Empirical Researches in Urban Management, 2*(11), 64–79. Available: http://www.um.ase.ro.

Affaki, M. S. (2021). Reconstruction of heritage and spirit: Mending the scars of aleppo. In F.F. Arefian, J. Ryser, A. Hopkins, & J. Mackee (Eds.), *Historic cities in the face of disasters. The urban book series*. Springer, Cham. https://doi.org/10.1007/978-3-030-77356-4_15

Akkermans, P. M. M. G., & Schwartz, G. M. (2003). *The archaeology of syria from complex hunter-gatherers to early urban societies (ca 16,000–300 BC)*. Cambridge University Press.

Akkoc, R. (2016). What has been the real cost of Ssyria's civil war? Retrieved 2020, from https://www.telegraph.co.uk/news/worldnews/middleeeast/syria/12146082/What-has-been-the-real-cost-of-syrias-civil-war.html.

Annan, D. (2019). Post-conflict reconstruction and development findings in ... Retrieved from https://www.researchgate.net/publication/336170672_POST-CONFLICT_RECONSTRUCTION_AND_DEVELOPMENT_FINDINGS_IN_SOUTH_SUDAN

Arefian, F. F. (2018). A synthesise of multidisciplinary theoretical discussions. In *Organising Post-Disaster Reconstruction Processes. The Urban Book Series*. Springer, Cham. https://doi.org/10.1007/978-3-319-70911-6_2

Arefian, F. F. (2021). Pre-disaster examination as post-disaster managerial thinking ahead for Hoi An, Vietnam. In F. F. Arefian, J. Ryser, A. Hopkins, & J. Mackee (Eds.), *Historic cities in the face of disasters. The Urban Book Series*. Springer, Cham. https://doi.org/10.1007/978-3-030-77356-4_21

Azzouz, A. (2019). A tale of a Syrian city at war. *City, 23*(1), 107–122. https://doi.org/10.1080/13604813.2019.1575605

Berman, M. (1983). *All that is solid melts into air: The experience of modernity*. Verso.

Berman, M. (2018). *Emerging from the ruins*. Dissent Magazine. Retrieved from https://www.dissentmagazine.org/article/emerging-from-the-ruins.

Bexar. (2020). The five phases of emergency management. Retrieved April, 2020, from https://www.bexar.org/694/Five-Phases

Brun, C., & Lund, R. (2008). Making a home during crisis: Post-tsunami recovery in a context of war, Sri Lanka. *Singapore Journal of Tropical Geography*. https://doi.org/10.1111/j.1467-9493.2008.00334.x

Camagni, R. (2017) Integrated spatial planning: Why and how?. In R. Capello (Eds.), *Seminal studies in regional and urban economics*. Springer, Cham. https://doi.org/10.1007/978-3-319-57807-1_19

Cattaneo, B. (2020). How our planet became more urbanised than ever. Retrieved

Caves, R. W. (2004). Encyclopedia of the city (pp. 704). Routledge. ISBN 978–0415862875.

CCAHA. (2020). Emergency management cycle. Retrieved April, 2020, from https://ccaha.org/res ources/emergency-management-cycle
Counsell, D., Allmendinger, P., Haughton, G., & Vigar, G. (2006). Integrated spatial planning: Is it living up to expectations?. *Town and Country Planning 75*(9), 243–246.
Coward, M. (2009). *Urbicide: The politics of urban destruction*. Taylor and Francis.
Coward, M. (2010). Urbicide: The politics of urban destruction by Martin Coward. Retrieved March, 2020, from https://www.researchgate.net/publication/270847619_Urbicide_The_Pol itics_of_Urban_Destruction_By_Martin_Coward
CSIS & AUSA. (2002). *Postconflict reconstruction task framework*. https://csis-prod.s3.amazon aws.com/s3fs-public/legacy_files/files/media/csis/pubs/framework.pdf
Davis, M. (2002). *City of quartz: Excavating the future in Los Angeles*. Vintage Books.
De Rooij, B., Wascher, D., & Paulissen, M. (n.d.). *Sustainable design principles for refugee camps*. Wageningen University and research.
Doppelhofer, Ch., (2016). Will Palmyra rise again?—War crimes against cultural heritage and post-war reconstruction. [online] http://www.ohchr.org/EN/Issues/CulturalRights/Pages/IntentionalD estruction.aspx
Douglas Porteous, J., & Smith, S. E. (2003). Domicide: The global destruction of home. *Housing Studies, 18*(2), 269–272. https://doi.org/10.1080/0267303032000087766
Earnest, J. (2015). Postconflict reconstruction—A case study in Kosovo: The complexity of planning and implementing infrastructure projects. *International Journal of Emergency Services, 4*, 103.
Etaywe, A. (2017). The logic of urbicidal terrorism and its implications on the protection of civilians: Lessons to be learned from Syria. Retrieved 2020, from https://www.researchgate.net/ publication/326000071_The_Logic_of_Urbicidal_Terrorism_and_Its_Implications_on_the_ Protection_of_Civilians_Lessons_to_be_Learned_from_Syria
FEMA. (2004). Emergency management in the United States. Retrieved from https://training.fema. gov/emiweb/downloads/is111_unit%204.pdf
FEMA. (2009). National disaster housing strategy. Retrieved from https://www.fema.gov/pdf/eme rgency/disasterhousing/NDHS-core.pdf
Fracolli, L. A., Zoboli, E. L. P., Granja, G. F., & Ermel, R. C. (2011). The concept and practice of comprehensiveness in primary health care: Nurses' perception. *Revista Da Escola De Enfermagem Da U.s.p., 45*(5), 1135–1141.
Francis, D. J. (2016). *Timing and sequencing of postconflict reconstruction and peacebuilding efforts in South Sudan*. In A. Langer, & G. K. Brown (Eds.), *Building sustainable peace: Timing and sequencing of postconflict reconstruction and peacebuilding*. Oxford University Press.
Goldman, M. (2015). Development and the City. In F. Miraftab & N. Kudva (Eds.), *Cities of the global south reader* (pp. 54–65). Routledge.
Goodson, L. (2001). *Afghanistan's endless war: State failure, regional politics, and the rise of the taliban*. University of Washington Press.
Grodach, C. (2002). Reconstituting identity and history in post-war mostar, Bosnia-Herzegovina. *City, 6*(1), 61–82.
Henkey, T. (2018). *Urban emergency management: planning and response for the 21st century*. Butterworth-Heinemann.
Huxtable, A. (1972). *Will they ever finish bruckner boulevard?* Collier Books.
IISS. (2017). *Armed conflict in cities: Humanitarian implications and responses* (Rep.).
Jazeera, A. (2017). Syria's civil war explained from the beginning. Retrieved 2020, from http:// www.aljazeera.com/news/2016/05/syria
Kanjou, Y. (2018). The role of the local community and museums in the renaissance of Syrian cultural heritage. *Journal of Eastern Mediterranean Archaeology & Heritage Studies, 6*(4), 375–391. Retrieved 2020, from https://www.jstor.org/stable/10.5325/jeasmedarcherstu.6.4.0375
Karasapan, O., Syria's mental health crisis, Brookings, (2015), https://www.brookings.edu/blog/fut uredevelopment/2016/04/25/syrias-mental-health-crisis
Kostof, S., & Tobias, R. (1999). *The city shaped: Urban patterns and meanings through history*. Thames & Hudson.

References

Lefebvre, H. (2016). *The production of space*. Blackwell.

Lotfi, S., & Solaimani, K. (2009). An assessment of urban quality of life by using analytic hierarchy process approach (case study: Comparative study of quality of life in the North of Iran). *Journal of Social Sciences, 5*(2), 123–133.

MacCallum, D., Babb, C., & Curtis, C. (2019). *Doing research in urban and regional planning: Lessons in practical methods*. Routledge.

Macrorie, R., & Marvin, S. (2019). Bifurcated urban integration: The selective dis- and re-assembly of infrastructures. *Urban Studies, 56*. https://doi.org/10.1177/0042098018812728

Mahfouz, J. (2021) Old souks of Aleppo: A narrative approach to post-conflict heritage reconstruction. In F.F. Arefian, J. Ryser, A. Hopkins, J. Mackee (Eds.), *Historic Cities in the Face of Disasters. The Urban Book Series*. Springer, Cham. https://doi.org/10.1007/978-3-030-77356-4_3

McArthur, D. (2018). Book review: Urban emergency management. ASIS Homepage. Retrieved from https://www.asisonline.org/security-management-magazine/articles/2018/12/book-review-urban-emergency-management/

McKenzie, W., & Oliver, G. (2018, March 15). How seven years of war turned Syria's cities into 'hell on Earth'. Retrieved March, 2020, from https://edition.cnn.com/2018/03/15/middleeast/syria-then-now-satellite-intl/index.html

Milojevic, B. (2018, June). Integrated urban planning in theory and practice. Retrieved 2020, from https://www.researchgate.net/publication/325714737_INTEGRATED_URBAN_PLANNING_IN_THEORY_AND_PRACTICE

Mishchuk, H., & Grishnova, O. (2015). Empirical study of the comfort of living and working environment—Ukraine and Europe: Comparative assessment. *Journal of International Studies, 8*(1), 67–80. https://doi.org/10.14254/2071-8330.2015/8-1/6

Moorcock, M. (1963). Dead god's homecoming. Retrieved March, 2020, from http://www.eclipse.co.uk/sweetdespise/moorcock/bib/short/dgh.html

NEPAD. (2005). 'African postconflict reconstruction policy framework', New Partnership for Africa's Developent (NEPAD) Secretariat, Governance, Peace and Security Programme, South Africa.

O'Driscoll, D. (2018). *Postconflict Reconstruction Good Practice*. K4D Helpdesk, Brighton, UK: Institute of Development Studies.

OCCHA. (2017). 2017 Humanitarian needs overview: Syrian Arab Republic [EN/AR] - Syrian Arab Republic. Retrieved, 2020, from https://reliefweb.int/report/syrian-arab-republic/2017-humanitarian-needs-overview-syrian-arab-republic-enar

Pineo, H., & Rydin, Y. (2018). Cities, health and well-being. *The royal institution of chartered surveyors (RICS)*, 1–40; Rawles, J. (2016). Developing social work professional judgment skills: enhancing learning in practice by researching learning in practice. *Journal of Teaching in Social Work, 36*(1), 102–122. https://doi.org/10.1080/08841233.2016.1124004

Pugh, M. (1998). Post-conflict rehabilitation: The humanitarian ... - eth z. Retrieved from https://www.files.ethz.ch/isn/102390/1998_10_Post-Conflict_Rehabilitation.

REACH. (2019). 65% DAMAGED—A storm that redefined a country. Retrieved, 2020, from https://www.reach-initiative.org/what-we-do/news/65-damaged-a-storm-that-redefined-a-country

Rotondo, F., & Selocato, F. (2014). The role of G.I.S. for the industrial areas management to prevent the brownfields birth. The case of the Apulia Region in Southern Italy. In A. Djukic, M., Stankovic, B., Milojevic & N. Novakovic (Eds.), *Banjaluka Proceedings of international academic conference brown Info* (pp. 29–36), 1st edn: University of Banja Luka Faculty for Architecture, Civil Engineering and Geodesy.

Sakalasuriya, M. M., Haigh, R. P., & Amaratunga, D. (2018). A Conceptual framework to analyse consequences of postconflict reconstruction interventions. *Procedia Engineering, 212*, 894–901. https://doi.org/10.1016/j.proeng.2018.01.115

Serag El Din, H., Shalaby, A., Farouh, H. E., & Elariane, S. A. (2013). Principles of urban quality of life for a neighborhood. *Hbrc Journal, 9*(1), 86–92. https://doi.org/10.1016/j.hbrcj.2013.02.007

Takla, F. (2020). Marota city. Retrieved April, 2020, from http://www.fouadtakla.com/Update/Focus/Article/8

Taylor, N. (1998). *Urban planning theory since 1945* (pp. 3–4). Sage. ISBN 978–0–7619–6093–5.

Theron, S. (2011). Postconflict reconstruction: The case of ethnicity in Burundi. *Insight on Africa, 3*, 143–158.

Tornberg, P. (2011). Making sense of integrated planning; challenges to urban and transport planning processes in Sweden. Retrieved 2020, from https://www.divaportal.org/smash/get/diva2:459001/FULLTEXT03.pdf

UN-Habitat. (2016). UN-Habitat III—New urban agenda, Quito. [Online]. Available: www.habitat3.org/the-new-urban-agenda, [15.01.2018].

UN-Habitat. (2017). *Good practices and lessons learned in postconflict reconstruction in Sri Lanka*. UN-Habitat Report. http://unhabitat.lk/wp-content/uploads/2017/10/Good-practices-and-lessons-learned_Final-003.pdf

UN-Habitat. (2017). The new urban agenda. Retrieved February, 2020, from https://habitat3.org/the-new-urban-agenda/

UN-Habitat. (2020). The new urban agenda. Retrieved, 2020, from https://habitat3.org/the-new-urban-agenda/.

UNDP. (2013). Community based resilience analysis (CoBRA): Conceptual framework and methodology. United Nations Development Programme (UNDP) Drylands Development Centre. Retrieved from http://www.undp.org/content/dam/undp/library/Environment%20and%20Energy/sustainable%20land%20management/CoBRA/CoBRRA_Conceptual_Framework.pdf

UNDP. (2020a). Community based resilience analysis (CoBRA): Conceptual framework and methodology. United Nations Development Programme (UNDP) Drylands Development Centre. Retrieved from http://www.undp.org.

UNDP. (2020b). Goal 11: Sustainable cities and communities. Retrieved February, 2020b, from https://www.undp.org/content/undp/en/home/sustainable-development-goals/goal-11-sustainable-cities-and-communities.html

UNHCR. (2020). Voluntary returns of Syrian refugees: Regional analysis. Retrieved 2020, from https://data2.unhcr.org/en/

UNITAR-UNOSAT. (2015), Four years of human suffering—The Syria conflict as observed through satellite imagery.

UNITAR. (2020). Syria World Heritage Sites Report. Retrieved, 2020, from https://unitar.org/sustainable-development-goals/satellite-analysis-and-applied-research/chs-syria

Urbandictionary. (2020). Urbicide. Retrieved February 03, 2020, from https://www.urbandictionary.com/define.php?term=urbicide

Visser, G. (2001). Social justice, integrated development planning and post-apartheid urban reconstruction. *Urban Studies, 38*(10), 1673–1699.

World Vision. (2020, March 06). Fears and Dreams of Syrian children. Retrieved, 2020, from https://www.wvi.org/fearsanddreamscontinued/

WorldBank. (2017). The toll of war: The economic and social consequences of the conflict in Syria. Online: http://www.worldbank.org/en/country/syria/publication/the-toll-of-war-the-economic-and-social-consequences-of-the-conflict-in-syria retrieved 31–04–2020.

Yigitcanlar, & Teriman, S. (2014). Rethinking sustainable urban development: Towards an integrated planning and development process. *International Journal of Environmental Science and Technology, 12*(1), 341–352.

Chapter 3
Spaces in Emergency

Abstract This chapter analyzes the two selected case studies, namely, Damascus city in Syria and Zaatari refugee camp in Jordan. The chapter first investigates the direct urbicide in Damascus city through analyzing its urban development; studying the distribution of the informal settlements in Damascus; understanding Damascus urban scenario in wartime; exploring the Syrian approach in construction and discussing the organization laws in Syria, including the law 10, the Law No. 33, the Law 9. It analyzes the damage, especially in the housing sector in an aim to determine the real need for the city. The second section analyzes the indirect urbicide in Zaatari refugee camp in Jordan. It discusses the urban scenario, the laws and regulations that govern building construction and urban planning in the country, such as Municipality law no 29 for 1955 Law of Planning Cities; Towns Villages and Buildings No. 79 for the year 1966 on Planning and building regulations; Jordan National Building Law no. 7/93; Antiquity Law No. 21 for the Year 1988 of Antiquities and Archaeology; Law no. 21/1971—Public Health; Law no. 1 of 2003 Environmental Protection; Agricultural Law No. 20, 1973 and the Amman building and urban planning regulation of 2011. Then, it discusses the population growth and investigates the Zaatari camp from urban housing perspective, not as an abrupt space for an emergency.

Keywords Direct urbicide · Indirect urbicide · Damascus · Zaatari

3.1 Direct Urbicide: Damascus City in Syria

The Syrian Civil War has entered its tenth year since 15 March 2011. As the capital, Damascus has been deeply impacted by the heavy fighting that happened all over the country. There is inevitably a certain amount of overlapping challenges. First, Damascus had the largest share of internally displaced people from conflict areas, especially from Deir Ezzor and Raqqa, who fled to the eastern districts of Damascus. Secondly, the destruction in the east and southeast parts of the city, 80% of east and western Ghouta, has been destroyed. Thirdly, the state of random housing, informal settlements, and refugee camps in Damascus existed before the Syrian Civil War, (30–40) % of housing around the major cities are slums. Fourthly, the real state laws, and the construction laws like law 10, Decree (60, 61, 62, 66, 107). Lastly, Damascus master plan before 2011, the land division, and ownership issues.

As warfare's geography has rearranged house-holds across space, it is essential to study Damascus's spatial and organizational development. Consequently, this chapter will present Damascus's spatial planning and geographic structure; Damascus land uses and spreads of the informal settlements; the construction acts and decrees; and Damascus damage assessment.

3.1.1 The Urban Development of Damascus

Damascus, Dimashq, the city of Jasmine, the pearl of the East or Alsham, no matter how many names but one fact that it is one of the important cultural centers of the Levant and the Arab World. It is considered one of the oldest contentiously inhabited cities. The evidence of inhabitation is dated back to 5000 B.C, in the fertile Ghouta oasis on the river of Barada and in the junction of the trade center (Eldredge et al., 2014). As Bonine (1977, p.141) said: "in many regions of the world, one views urbanism in terms of centuries, whereas in Syria, millennia are more appropriate."

The urban morphology of Damascus has been changed over the years; consequently, the transformation on Damascus planning could be analyzed and studied based on the different civilization that crossed it: the early ancient Damascus (5000 BC–64 BC); the Islamic Damascus (635 AD–1516 AD); the Ottoman Damascus (1516 AD–1916 AD); Damascus city under the French Mandate (1916–1948); Damascus city after the independence (1948); Damascus under the Baath socialist (1948–1963); Damascus and Ecochard traffic plan (the 1970s); the Urbanized Damascus (1982–2012); and Damascus city under conflict (2012–up to now).

It is essential to address a city's urban transformation like Damascus, which unfolds multiple historical metamorphoses since what happened before and what is happening now will lead us to create a comprehensive reconstruction vision for such a city with a profound history and to achieve integrated spatial planning policy that able to regenerate a city with urban identity.

3.1.2 From a Strong Classical Geometric Pattern to a Compact Organic Urban Form: Greco-Roman Damascus and Islamic Damascus Urban Matrix

A real city planning and aboriginal urban form started to be noticed after the arrival of Alexander the Great on 333 BC, on this period, the city of Damascus resembled a small Greek city with grid-streets networks, Agora and the temple of Zeus as it was described by Bonine (1977) as a city with wide streets that led to a collective of public buildings, consequently, the Hellenic period had a clear contribution in shaping the

3.1 Direct Urbicide: Damascus City in Syria

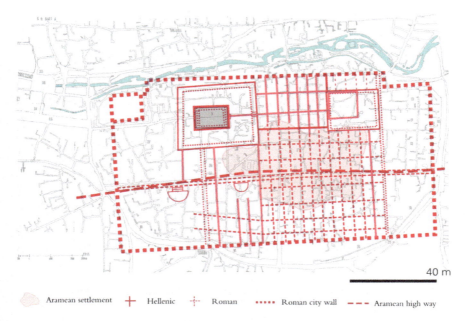

Fig. 3.1 The roman damascus 64 BC. Ref: ETH Studio Basel, 2009

morphological legacy of Damascus (Lababedi, 2008). By the end of Hellenistic rule and the beginning of the Roman empire, Damascus continued its expansion on the grid plan as a gated city surrounded by a rectangular stone wall with seven gates as illustrated in Fig. 3.1.

Roman and Greek planning has influenced Damascus's city planning up to today. The city cropped up based on the Roman plan so that the Old Town of Damascus maintains a rectangular form with the existence of the two main axes: the Cardo (north–south) and the Decumanus Maximus (east–west) Via Recta (UNESCO, 2019), which is recognized now as Medhat Pasha Street (ICOMOS, 2008) running from Bab Sharqi to Bab-Al-Jabiya—two still-standing gates of the seven Roman gates (Lababedi, 2008). One can see the Old Town plan of 1919 is based on the Roman plan, illustrated in Fig. 3.2. Moreover, the city was oriented according to the Greek city, and therefore all its streets are directed aligned north–south or east–west (UNESCO, 2019).

As a result of the siege of Damascus 634 AD, Damascus fell under Muslim conquest (Akram, 2004), upon that, the city planning deformed gradually and slowly into more organic forms, far from the Greek and Romans strong geometric patterns and it grew out of the Roman wall. Islam rituals, thoughts, and believes were the leaders of the transmogrification from the Roman wide grid street patterns with forums to Islamic urban compacted urban form, narrow streets with the absence of large public spaces (ETH, 2012). As Fig. 3.3 shows the transformation from a chess

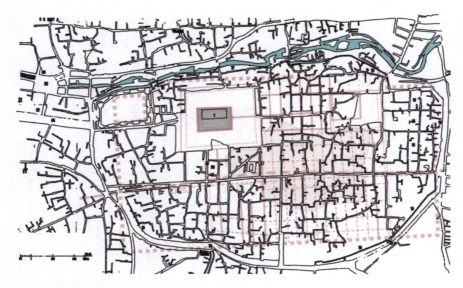

Fig. 3.2 The old town 1919 based on the roman plan. Ref: ETH Studio Basel, 2009

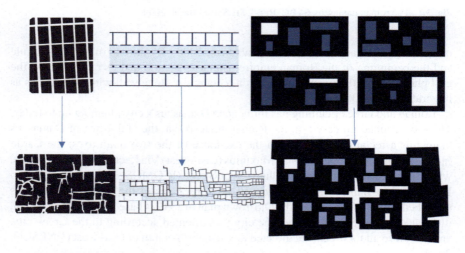

Fig. 3.3 The urban transmogrification from the classical Greco-Roman Damascus to the Islamic Damascus. Ref: by the author from ETH Studio Basel, 2019

street Roman pattern into more spontaneous network and the reformation of the main Roman Cardo into Arabic market (Mansour, 2016).

Damascus flourished as an exemplary model of Arab-Muslim city and a capital for Umayyad Caliphate (UNESCO, 2019) with the presence of Umayyad Great Mosque at the core of the Greco-Roman grid urban pattern (UNESCO, 2019). On 750 A.D, the

Abbasid Caliphate moved the capital of Islamic state from Damascus to Baghdad, that led to a decline in Damascus population which was conjoined to a political conflict between Umayyads and Abbasids, when Abbasids demolished most of the Umayyads buildings including the Great Mosque (ETH, 2012). During the Fatimids Caliphate, Damascus was a shattered city with bad living conditions as the Arab Geographer "Al-Muqaddasi" described his visit to Damascus on 970 A.D "the city architecture and infrastructure was magnificent but the living conditions were awful" (Burns, 2005, pp. 137–138), by the end of twelfth century the city embraced more than 242 mosques (ETH, 2012). The better levels of safety and security during the Ayyubids Caliphate 1154 A.D promoted an "extra Muros" expansions (UNESCO, 2019) where Damascenes lived in satellite suburbs such as: Salihiyah at the base of Gassioun Mountain, Maydan in the southwest, Saruja in the north, and Amara in the north–west (Lababedi, 2008). As Burns (2005) described this period, which unfolded the first Islamic comprehensive town planning of Damascus, as "the city golden age" (p. 158) since the city's buildings were incomparable to any previous reconstructions, meticulous regenerations works devoted to improve Damascus Old City, especially, its public infrastructure which had been undervalued for centuries, also different maintenance works had been applied to reinforce the Roman gates, and constructing hospitals and religious buildings.

3.1.3 Reviving the Geometric Master Plan Layout: The Ottoman Damascus and Damascus Under the French Mandate

The Ottoman Damascus grew as a city of religious and trade migrations, where the Hajj migrations and the trade voyages had notably impacted the urban expansion of Damascus. The Hajj migration or "pilgrimage migration," which is the annual Islamic pilgrimage to Mecca "the holiest city for Muslims" deformed Damascus urban metamorphosis in two ways: firstly, the city sprouted to south along the route to Mecca, since Damascus was the major gathering point for pilgrims and caravans (ETH, 2012) to proceed their holy trip to Mecca, the number of pilgrims astonishingly accelerated due to the expansion of the Ottomans' power. Consequently, the Maydan district of Damascus hosted 25,000–60,000 pilgrims twice a year. For this reason, Maydan district flourished and was highly activated as a residential suburb and the development followed the south route toward Mecca, according to Burn (2005) extra Muros settlements had been almost tripled under the Ottoman empire from 0.64 km^2 to 1.84 km^2 within three centuries. Secondly, the city population increased 30% by migrants and that led to a quick expansion toward the suburbs (ETH, 2012). From the other side, trade voyages also impacted the expansion of the Ottoman Damascus, where the city received, yearly, two or three caravans of more than 2000 camels with their merchants (Arnaud, 2006).

The rule of the Ottoman Empire between the late of nineteenth century and the beginning of the twentieth century, the latest sixty years of Ottomans predominanc in Damascus, was considered as the reorganization period or as it was called "Tanzimat period" (Burns, 2000). During that time, Damascus had been impacted by important transformations with new administrative modalities of development and modernization of the urban space (Arnaud, 2006), the new urbanism concepts, that outlined by Grand Vizier Mustafa Rashid Pasha were inspired by the western European urban models, and he asked for the experience exchange with the western world through bringing European architects and urbanists to develop plans for Damascus and other Ottoman cities and to send Ottoman students abroad to learn the European methods and techniques in architecture and city planning ((Lababedi, 2008). The new urban model of Damascus, which had been developed during the Tanzimat period had three main concepts: to widen the street networks and to remove dead ends and cul-de-sacs, the new suburbs were designed within a geometric pattern, and a shift in the construction materials from wood to stone as a more fire resistance alternative in an aim to more durable construction (ETH, 2012). For example, in 1894, the first pre-planned residential neighborhood under the Ottoman rule "Al-Muhajirin" quarter, literally mean the refugees, was planned to accommodate the Christian and Muslim refugees who were massacred as a result of 1860 Civil War in Syria, which was the peak of a peasant uprising, which started in the north of the mount of Lebanon as a revolution of Marouite "Christians of Syrian origins" against their Druze overlords (Fawaz, 1994). The new quarter was located on a steep slope where the plots were divided into grid plan of 400 m^2 parcels, the refugees were offered with a high quality, large plots land in low price (Arnaud, 2006). Figure 3.4 shows the historical expansion of Damascus during the Roman period, the Ayyubids, Mamluki, and Ottomans.

The urban expansion of Damascus was mainly toward the south, on the right bank of Barada river, during the nineteenth century, while the population of Damascus had doubled, the demand on land had been increased, consequently, the city expanded 25% in area, specifically, from the old city walls, to south, headed to Maydan suburb and to north and north west along the way to Saruja (Lababeidi, 2008). By the end of the Ottoman rule, the major expansions were on the left bank of the river and toward the north, as could be seen in Fig. 3.5, because of the water resources availability through canals in the northern parts of Al-Ghouta (Fries, 2000).

Correspondingly, the urban density of Damascus had gradually increased, since the residents were attracted by the new planned residential suburbs served with wide streets and wide-ranging gardens and public parks. As Arnaud (2006) stated, paradoxically to the common belief, that Damascus planned and developed through the city planners works before the French mandates. And it demonstrated on high levels of modernity and European inspiration (Fries, 2000) such as: three train stations, electric tramways, traffic lights, and different buildings were erected in the new suburbs like: large hotels, theaters, cafes, schools, hospitals, and the first Syrian university. Some of these buildings had a notable manifestation of modern western style since they were designed by Italian and French architects who presented the Classical and Rococo style to Damascus buildings (Bianca, 2000).

3.1 Direct Urbicide: Damascus City in Syria

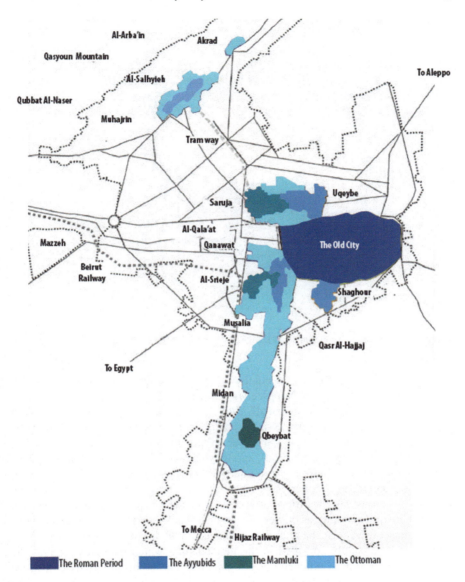

Fig. 3.4 The historical expansion of Damascus. by the author 2020

On the other side, public works were overlooked as Mo'ez (1968) indicated to the slow and poor improvements to the city infrastructure, such as, the construction of Beirut-Damascus road which took ten years to be completed. The Old City of Damascus at the end of Ottoman period witnessed a clear change on the social demographic strata as a result of the emigrations of the wealthier residents to the

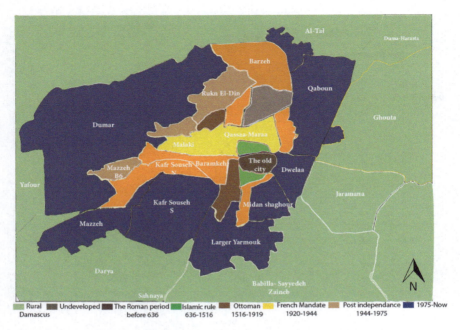

Fig. 3.5 The historical development of Damascus. Own illustration 2020

new suburbs, which deformed the quality of the old city structure into a deteriorated one, inhabited by the poorer Damascenes (Lababeidi, 2008).

After the First World War and dividing the Ottoman Empire between Britain and France (Myers, 1921), the Syrian territories went under the French Mandate who sought to proceed with the urban development that already had launched in the nineteenth century (Fries, 2000), and they created unprecedented master plans, neglecting the local culture, context, and traditions, as Hopwood (1988) described "the French entered as conquerors not as enlightened guests bearing the banner of the League of Nations" (P. 23). Apparently, French planners evaded any developments in the Old City of Damascus, as they considered it a "backward place for the indigenous Arabs" since the Mandate had a clear actual concern: to dominate the territory (Fries, 2000) and that plainly appeared in the new suburbs which explicitly express the French modern eastern influence in city planning and architectural style such as: boulevards, radio centric roads system, street networks, functional zoning, and so on, as Fries (1994) said that the city of Damascus resembled an "experimental field of French urbanism" showing a plan of that integrates "the universal idea of modernity" (P. 313).

Urban infrastructure and public works had been ignored, as discussed before, and that left the city in poor conditions. Consequently, the first French master plan for Damascus, shown in Fig. 3.6 was outlined, in 1935, by Rene Danger, handled

3.1 Direct Urbicide: Damascus City in Syria 71

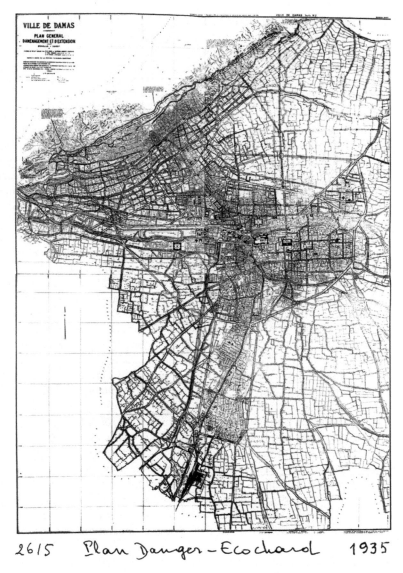

Fig. 3.6 The French urbanism in the middle east Danger-Ecochart Plan 1935. Ref: Aga Khan trust for culture, 2020

basically, the hygiene and infrastructure issues, and looked toward beautification of the city in a more western style (ETH, 2012).

The dissension of the new very western master plans from the local Damascenes, and the strict bureaucracy left over from Ottomans were considered by Danger master plan proposal, in order to move step forward in French urbanism in Damascus. It is worth mentioning that French urbanism was not restricted to territories that experienced French Colonialism, such as Syria and Lebanon, but also in other countries like Egypt, which witnessed British Colonialism (Njoh, 2015). The changes in Syria were difficult in the first ten years of the French Mandate (Fries, 2000). In addition to his comprehensive vision on city formation and transformation, as Danger explained (quoted in Fries, 1994, P. 135) "the various forms of cities…correspond to an environment physically, ethnographically, socially, and historically differ. All have their physiognomy and their own personality." Danges followed Lucien Vilbert experience in Morocco and his concept of a "dichotomy" to segregate the old indigenous city from the modern European city to maintain social, economic, and historical balance (Lababeidi, 2008) and drove the old city toward deterioration and neglect. Danger also worked with Michel Ecochard in a non-erected proposal, to improve the city streets networks to ease the congestion problem through radio centric road system and encircling the Old City with ring road (Elsa Wifstrand, 2018).

Danger and Ecochard had not only worked on a holistic framework for Damascus urban management but they designed a "morphological-functional zoning" of the city (Kallaa, 1993), which was approved in the 1960s and finished in 1994.

The urbanism issue in Damascus between 1919 and 1925 was the main tool to express Arabs' new political agendas and the rising Arab nationalism and rebellions against the illegitimate Ottoman rule. As Fries (2000, p. 157) described, "The city became the theater of national demonstrations where the urban form and the urbanism plan became the tools of power." On the one hand, evidence shows that after 1919, the Damascenes broke the Ottoman land codes and began constructing without government authorization. Thirty-six percent of Damascene houses were built without permits. Consequently, the city grew approximately 25% between 1920 and 1930, on top of its expansion over the previous 50 years (Fries, 2000). On the other hand, as evidence, Souq Sarouja literally means "Sarouja Market," which was considered the resistant movement headquarters, but it was wiped out with the aim of destroying the social militant issue (Kallaa, 1993). It transformed into a garden city with wide boulevards near to the mandate administration and served as "the economic administration center." In the latest half of the French Mandate, Ecochard shifted away from Danger's comprehensive approach toward the city and he focused on the value of the historical monuments as an important part in the city urban affairs, in which the new target was the historical monuments rather than controlling the city development.

In 1968, the French architect Michel Ecochard designed the Damascus master plan, as illustrated in Fig. 3.7, based on a pure functional town planning principle that stemmed from the Athens charter. Damascus' 1986 master plan linked different historical, hydrological, and demographical components considering street networks and regional planning elements that provide desirable services and protect the environment, particularly the water resources of Damascus Al-Ghouta. As a result, the expansion developed to the South–West of Damascus, Mezzah, and the airport region (Abdulac, 1982). The Ecochard plan introduced a new road system with encircling the old city with a ring road to lower the congestion. It also proposed new function zoning outside the old city with new sewage systems (Wifstrand, 2018).

3.1 Direct Urbicide: Damascus City in Syria

Fig. 3.7 1968 master plan for Damascus. Ref: Archnet, 2020

3.1.4 Informal Settlements in Damascus

Damascus witnessed a notable population growth, mainly outside the old city borders, after 1950 because of the influx of Palestinian refugees which has deeply impacted the city urban fabric and led to the formation of the illegal housing settlements. For instance, in Al-Ghouta region one of three residences is illegal squatter. The city of Damascus has rapidly grown especially after 2002 when Iraqi refugees came and settle in Jaramana which includes more than 13 illegal housing settlements (Wifstrand, 2018).

The dramatical population growth was accompanied by the population movement from the countryside to the major cities' center and since this increase was not organized through appropriate planning strategies or absorbed through a well-studied expansion of the existing organized zones which led to the spread of the random housing phenomenon all around Syria and in the surrounded areas of Damascus.

According to the Syrian Housing Minister's declaration in 2018, the informal housing settlements shape 40–50% of the inhabited zones (Hamedi, 2018). Between 1981 and 1994, the percentage of informal housing exceeded half of the total settlements, and in Damascus, precisely, the percentage of informal housing surpassed 67% (Jbour, 2002).

Fig. 3.8 Damascus ethnics distribution| By the author, 2020

The abrupt emergence of the informal settlements phenomenon in Syria has been connected (Fig. 3.8).

Different factors have contributed to shaping these informal settlements. Such as firstly: the population shifted from rural areas to urban centers, especially Damascus since it is the capital. Secondly, the Palestinian exodus after "Al-Nakbeh" in 1948 and after the Six-Days War "Al-Nakseh" in 1967, and the Al-Tahrir War in 1973. Thirdly: the implemented planning strategies, methods, and techniques failed to absorb the refugees' influx and face the urbanization phenomenon. See Fig. 3.9.

The informal settlements spread in the vicinity of Damascus, on the agricultural lands in Al-Ghouta and the mount Qassioun zone, as illustrated in Fig. 3.9. In the Al-Ghouta zone, the expansion of informalities started from the mid of 1950s near Qaboun and Joubar. In Mount Qassioun, the informal settlements pattern shaped a longitudinal strip that continued to stretch in the beginnings of the 1950s in Al-Muhajireen and Rukn Al-Din zone. In the 1970s, the expansion of the informal settlements reached Barza and Qudusyiah and by the beginnings of the 1980s, the informalities sprawled to Dumar and Mezzeh. The first law coped with the informal settlements issue was outlined in 1960 "the squatters and informalities" which is known as article 44 that formulated based on article 118 of the law no. 172 of 1956, which defined the informal settlement as any property that isn't in compliance with the approved master plan; any building that isn't in safe conditions or may collapse because of the absence of the strong structure based on a report from the technical department; or any building that located completely or partially in the public property (Khadour & Kafa, 2009).

3.1 Direct Urbicide: Damascus City in Syria

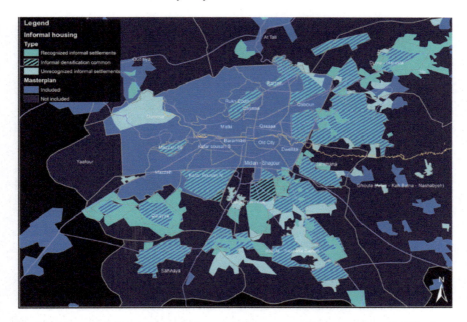

Fig. 3.9 The spread of the informal settlements in Damascus and its surroundings. Ref: Re-drawn by the author from Wind & Ibrahim 2020

Khadour & Kafa (2009) mentioned that the informal urban fabric in Damascus is "a patchwork of unplanned buildings" which had been accidentally emerged without any connection to Damascus urban fabric or the Damascene architectural identity. The arrangement of the informal settlements changed based on the land topography. Consequently, their composition shapes either a grid pattern, as in Al-Tabaleh eastern Damascus and Al-Kadam southern Damascus, or an organic one as Mezzeh in northwest Damascus. As could be seen in Fig. 3.10. The grid fabric consists of 10–12 * 8 m land sections in which each of them is divided into smaller plots for house units served with small networks of roads and Cul-De-sacs.

The informal construction has dramatically increased in the first period of the Syrian Civil War, precisely, between 2011 and 2013, especially in the rebel-controlled urban fringe (Clerc, 2014), which are approximately the districts situated on the eastern side of the old city. To name some: Qaboun, Jobar, Harasta, Irbin, Duma, Ghouta. The southern suburbs such as Darya, Kafr Souseh, Babilla, and Al-Yarmouk camp (Wind & Ibrahim, 2020).

Fig. 3.10 Informal settlements built on the slopes of mount Qassiun are overlooking the city center of Damascus. Photo V.Clerc 2009

3.2 Damascus Urban Scenario in Wartime

As one of the main Syrian cities, Damascus has been highly impacted by the Syrian civil war, either by physical destruction or human suffering through displacement. As stated by Wind and Ibrahim (2020) that "Syria's armed conflict left awful scars in Damascus's urban fabric and social structure." After 10 years of the Syrian civil conflict, since March 2011, the harsh fighting deeply hit Damascus's housing sector. From one side, the severe damage affected large parts of Damascus, particularly its eastern and southern fringes. From the other one, the mass inflow of the internally displaced to the undamaged districts of Damascus governorate. As mentioned in research interviews, people displaced from the areas under bombardment to the safer zones because the heavy fighting was exclusively concentrated in specific regions. Thus, we find an overpopulation in the governorates' centers, such as Damascus's city center, the center of the Latakia governorate, the center of the Aleppo governorate, the center of the Tartus governorate, and the central regions which are the middle coastal and southern regions. Consequently, the IDPs' exodus to the cities' centers has naturally contributed to a sudden and unpredictable increase in the population of Damascus. According to the United Nations world population prospects, the current population of Damascus 2020 is 2.3012.000 with an increase of 1.61 from 2019. As illustrated in Fig. 3.11.

Following the population demographics, one could notice the population change and the population growth rate between 2010 and 2020 in Damascus city. As shown in Table 3.1 and Fig. 3.12.

By the same token, an expert in the reconstruction field explained that although the issue of the population influx and internal displacement presents now in all the Syrian regions, Damascus had the largest share of the number of displaced persons, and it was the first chosen displacement destiny for most Syrians for different reasons: First of all, Damascus is the capital of the Syrian Republic; therefore, the most services are

3.2 Damascus Urban Scenario in Wartime

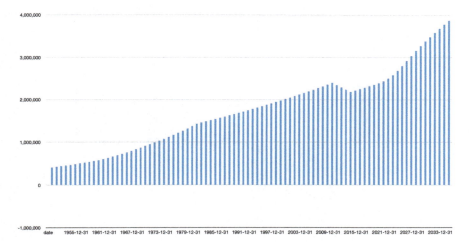

Fig. 3.11 Damascus population from 1950–2033. Ref: By the author form the United Nations World Population, 2021

Table 3.1 The change in the population and the growth rate in Damascus 2010–2035

Year	Population	Growth rate
2010	2,401,000	1.78
2011	2,346,000	−2.29
2012	2,293,000	−2.26
2013	2,242,000	−2.22
2014	2,191,000	−2.27
2015	2,223,000	1.46
2016	2,255,000	1.44
2017	2,287,000	1.42
2018	2,320,000	1.44
2019	2,354,000	1.47
2020	2,392,000	1.6
2035	3,873,000	2.41

Ref: Own illustration from the United Nations World Population

available and still operating, especially the educational services where people had a big concern to preserve their children's education process. Secondly, Damascus is the safest and the most secure zone, capable of accommodating the most significant number of people. Thirdly, some people don't like to emigrate outside the country for social or political reasons.

He also confirmed that the displacement flow pattern was not schematized and regulated. There are no camps or temporary random gatherings in Damascus or its surroundings, and in fact, people chose specific areas to flee to them. For example,

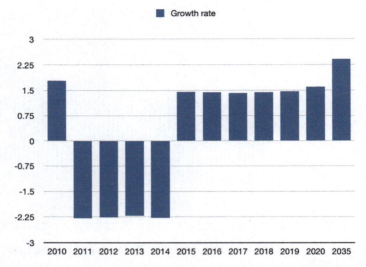

Fig. 3.12 Damascus population growth rate from 2010 to 2035. Ref: By the author from the United Nations World Population 2020

the eastern districts such as Jamara and Qudusiyeh had witnessed a massive IDP flow from Deir Ez-Zur and Raqqa. The Syrian from Raqqa and Deir Ez-Zur decided to flee to Jamara and Qudusiyeh because of the moderate living costs; the reasonable houses' rents, and the similarity of the lifestyle.

In reality, the intensity of displacement to Damascus and its surroundings began specifically in 2014 during the controlling period of ISIS over the Al-Jazeera region between 2014 and 2018. The 90% of the IDPs rented apartments in Damascus and its surroundings since they were financially stable. In comparison, 10% of them had been accommodated in Asylum centers, which were not socially accepted by the largest Syrian society segments, especially for the IDPs from the eastern regions, which are tribes. Therefore, this kind of temporary accommodation doesn't commensurate with their culture, society, customs, and traditions. As illustrated in Fig. 3.13.

Asylum center was not a widespread phenomenon in Damascus. Still, it was only notable through the use of the state facilities, the schools in particular, as they have been transformed into asylum centers. They were managed by national organizations such as the Syrian Arab Red Crescent and other social associations affiliated to the Ministry of Social Affairs to accommodate the most vulnerable families and provide them with basic services such as food, water, and health supplies. Apparently, these evacuation centers provided a temporary shelter for the stricken families as with the start of the school semester; they were forced to leave.

The implemented re-housing strategies in Damascus which were the private rental, squatting, and the asylum centers, as well as, the way in which Damascus absorbed the sudden influx of IDPs put the housing sector in a critical situation. From one side, the highly increased demand in the housing sector led to a ridiculous increase

3.2 Damascus Urban Scenario in Wartime

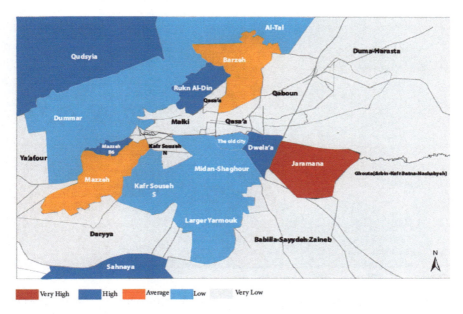

Fig. 3.13 The internally displaced persons in Damascus districts. By the author from Wind & Ibrahim, 2020

in rental prices. As explained by a Syrian displaced, who preferred not to mention his name, that he rented his house in Damascus after being displaced from Barzeh at the beginning of 2016 for an amount of 30,000 SYP, which is equal to 50.00 Euro, per month and by the end of the same year, the rent reaches 100,000 SYP, 167.00 Euro. Because of the increased demand for housing by the IDPs and the availability of alternative tenants. On the other side, Damascus didn't have more available places that can be rented. As discussed by Damascene homeowner, from his own experience in the neighborhood where he was living in 2014, during that period, an average of 10% of the houses in that area were empty. In comparison to now, where in the same neighborhood, each apartment accommodates, at minimum, two families with shared services such as the kitchen and bathrooms. This scenario is frequently repeated in Damascus, in which two families or more live together in the same house in which its area doesn't exceed 90 m^2. Remarkably, a housing paradox characterizes Damascus during the conflict. From one side, the number of vacant properties has increased because refugees and out-migrants had abandoned their real estates while the need and the demand for housing from IDPs is high. Consequently, the squatting phenomenon appeared almost in Damascus's districts, as illustrated in Fig. 3.14, especially in the eastern fringe of Damascus, such as Duma, Harasta, Arbin, and Yarmouk (Wind & Ibrahim, 2020).

In the same vein, a Syrian expert in urban studies confirmed that Damascus had received a considerable influx of IDPs at the beginning of the Syrian Civil War, especially in the Rural of Damascus "Rif Dimashq" because the capital's rent prices

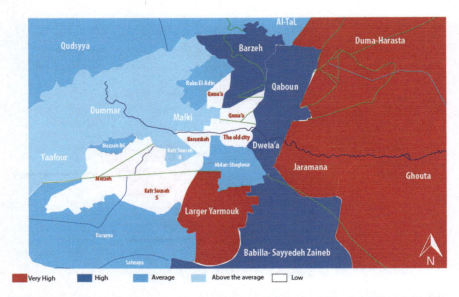

Fig. 3.14 Squatting in Damascus and its surroundings. Ref: by the author from Wind & Ibrahim, 2020

were very high. Based on his experience, he said that "one house's rent price in Damascus is equivalent to the rent of five houses in the countryside."

As a result, the significant number of displaced persons was not in Damascus's heart, but in the Rural Damascus, "Rif Dimashq." The lack of housing alternatives and the residential buildings' small areas contributed to escalating the rent prices in Damascus. Consequently, the financial conditions of the displaced persons impacted their choices. Those with the financial ability had rented in Damascus, in areas such as Al-Tal in the eastern region of Damascus and the Ma'araba area. In comparison, others fled to Damascus outskirts such as Sahnaya southern Damascus.

3.3 The Syrian Approach in Construction: An Eye Over the Organization Laws in Syria

The reconstruction of Syria is very complicated and requires collaborative efforts from the international political actors. From the one side, the cost of reconstruction works in Syria has been estimated in 2016 by the World Bank with an amount of 200 billion euros (Howard, 2019). In comparison, the United Nations estimations exceeded 200 billion euros (Calamur, 2019). In the World Bank last measures of 2019, their results revealed that rebuilding the country ranged from 200 billion euro to 350 billion euro (Daher, 2019). From the other side, any PRC agenda being developed, it should contribute to attaining justice between civilians. So, the critical aspect of this requires improvements to the country's housing, land, and property (HLP) rights (Baumann, 2019). Currently, in Syria, more than 1.7 million homes are destroyed or damaged (Hanna & Harastani, 2019).

There are different urban politics for the reconstruction in Syria, which have been outlined by the Syrian authorities. Such as Law 9, Decree 66, the new legal policy that launched in 2012, and law 10. Law 9 was legislated in 1975 and stated that "any cemented informal unit built on private land has the right to compensation regardless of the ownership." However, Law 9 Decree 66 fundamentally changed this legal identification of the informal patterns of property ownership that were the norm for many people (Hanna & Harastani, 2019). In April 2018, Decree 66 has been revised by the Syrian government to extend its applicability to the whole nation and is currently known as "Law 10." This Law allows award contracts of reconstruction to national and international investors, and to compensate citizens in the form of shares in regulatory zones (Friedrich-Eber, 2019). These laws demonstrate high levels of social injustice, as could be seen in the project of "Marota City," as shown in Fig. 3.15, which could be considered as an example of gentrification during post-conflict reconstruction. The project was initiated by the Syrian government in Damascus in 2012. Marota was a city of 6733 informal units; the new master plan aimed to replace the traditional patterns of informality in housing with a more modern plan (Hanna & Harastani, 2019) as Fig. 3.15 demonstrates. The new proposal includes 186 residential buildings with floor heights ranging from 11 to 22 floors, 33 commercial premises with some reaching 50 floors height, a shopping mall with a buildable area of 120,000 m^2, and other educational, governmental, and recreational facilities (Takla, 2020). The new project neglects Damascene culture and lifestyle.

Fig. 3.15 Marota city project. Ref: Takla (2020)

Marota City, according to Hanna (2019), could be considered a pilot city for the Post-conflict reconstruction in Syria. But, in fact, this kind of rehabilitation lacks identity and has no connection with the damascene culture and history.

In the reconstruction laws, as mentioned earlier, the redevelopment decisions are exclusively taken by the government, disregarding the importance of local participation and ignoring the social and cultural aspects, they are unfair in providing compensation and rehousing for many informal residents. For instance, Law 10 has different defects. First, it shapes a burden on refugees and IDPs in proofing their ownerships since it requires a specific procedure to claim their ownerships, which is exclusionary and not feasible. Second, it neglects the Damascene social and cultural background by stating the targeted area of reconstruction depends on the economic turnovers (Friedrich-Eber, 2019). And this will put local culture and heritage of the Damascene in great jeopardy of losing their cities' identity, as it happened with the Lebanese in Beirut downtown project "the New Solidere." Apparently, the " Solidere" model of reconstructing Beirut Downtown after the Lebanese Civil War (1975–1990) attracts many governments in the MENA region, despite the infinite critics of this reconstruction model, which is based on what so-called "disaster capitalism" in which the process of reconstruction led by private companies neglecting the role of citizens and local actors in rebuilding their neighborhoods (Elfeituri, 2021).

The Syrian civil war's political economy has changed the actors' power in urban planning and housing. Consequently, it is essential to discuss the land tenure, the spatial planning laws, and the reconstruction decrees to understand these laws' current situation and fill the gaps to attain better reconstruction and planning policy.

3.3.1 The Law 10

On April 2, 2018, the Syrian government issued Law 10, which permits planning zones throughout Syria dedicated to the reconstruction. Law 10 doesn't specify criteria for classifying the zones as an area to be organized or not and doesn't determine an exact timetable for the rebuilding. Still, rather zones are determined by a decree and within a week of issuing that decree to rebuild an area. The local authorities should request from the operating real estate agencies a list of the real estate owners in that area. Bodies must submit the lists within 45 days from the date of receiving the request.

The owners whose properties don't appear on the list will be notified to show up and prove their ownership within 30 days. In case they don't do so, they will not be compensated, and the property's ownership will revert to the town, city, or district where the property is located.

In case of proofing the property's ownership, the owners will have one of the three alternatives: First, register the subdivision in their names to get a share of the profits from the reconstruction. The second is to sell their share at auction. The third is to establish shareholder companies for investment reconstruction of the division. By this law, everyone residing in these areas is obliged to leave. The local authorities will provide compensation equivalent to two years' rent to the tenants who cannot reach an alternative housing. While tenants who have the right to alternative housing will be housed within four years, and till that time, they will be awarded an annual rental allowance. The law doesn't clarify who is eligible for alternative housing or how it will be determined.

Law 10 was issued based on Decree 66, signed by Al-Asad in 2012 (OHCHR, 2017). Decree 66 organized two development areas only in the ring, which surrounds Damascus province (Arfeh, 2016). The Syrian government implemented decree 66 intending to redevelop the informal housing and the slum areas in two areas in Damascus. However, analysts and journalists reported that the decree was used to expel the residents without any compensation or alternative housing (Nasers, 2018).

3.3.2 The Law No. 33

Law No. 33 was issued in 2008. Firstly, to confirm the ownership of the constructed real estate and parts of the non-built real estate in residential communities located within the region's boundaries. Secondly, to correct their descriptions and sort them either as a regular organization or irregular one. Based on this law, most of the informal settlements' constructed properties are common ownership. Consequently, this law came to remove this kind of common ownership, and in this way, these properties will be able to be correctly registered according to the rules of the real estate departments. Law No. 33 was issued based on Decree No. 166 of 1967 to remove the common ownership in the agricultural lands considering the differences in application between built-up areas and lands. This law gives an important role for the administrative units in the implementation stage as they are involved in adjusting the random housing conditions within the informal settlements' areas, especially after the issuance of Law No. /1/ of 2003, which includes dealing with the conditions of the buildings' violations which can be fully activated only after the properties' adjustments which was the main reason for outlining the Law No. 33 of 2008.

The main reasons for issuing this law were:

- The large numbers of collective buildings' infringements in most cities, districts, centers, and sub-districts in which scattered random residential buildings have become whole neighborhoods that lack many necessary facilities and cannot be implemented in the absence of organization. Real estate ownership of the properties on which these buildings were constructed.
- Multiple application of legislation and laws issued to address the reality of urban planning in all forms and the multiplicity of carrying out any process of secreting these properties.
- There is a difference between the registration documents of the real estate registry in these areas and the current reality of the properties based on them.
- These properties are still in their main owners' names, and their descriptions are still agricultural or wasteland. At the same time, they have turned into something

like small towns, and the ownership has practically changed so that the number of owners is several thousand instead of a few dozens.

3.3.3 Law 9

Law No. 9 issued on January 27, 1974. Article A discussed the issue of creating the organizational areas that should be applied by the administrative authority of the region which apply their regulations in the following two cases: Firstly, to the areas affected by natural incidents such as earthquakes and floods, or which were damaged as a result of wars or fires. Secondly, to areas in which the administrative authorities intend to implement a general organizational plan related to it. The created zone by a decree will have its own file which based on Article 10 (A) includes a recent detailed plan issued by the survey department which indicates the boundaries of the area and boundaries of each of the real estate, documenting the constructed buildings with tables for their areas. In part (B) a plan should be prepared by the administrative authorities and approved by the Secretariat of the survey and real estate improvement department, indicating the boundaries of the updated plots, the boundaries of the streets to be created or modified, the location, size, and shape of public spaces, parks, and public structures. In part (C) the methodology, techniques, and conditions of the urban, archaeological, and decorative measures were determined especially with regards to the setbacks between the buildings that must be left free of construction, the building heights, the architectural designs, the distribution of sewage, electricity, water, and telephone networks considering the region requirements. As mentioned by a Syrian expert in construction laws and legislations that the formation of the construction and reconstruction laws in Syria since 2015 doesn't consider the social angle as they had nothing related to the housing issue or how to absorb the sudden population influx.

In summary, the current and previous laws of redevelopment and construction in Syria have different gaps in terms of the project's scale, scope, and timeline. Apparently, there is a lack of a comprehensive nationwide program that specifies a set of guidelines for the redevelopment, which encompasses different stakeholders and links large geographical areas. The construction laws lack a specific timetable that determines the total time required for any project from planning to execution. Notably, they lack a strategic comprehensive plan that fulfills the community's needs, desires, goals, and aspirations, as noticed in the redevelopment projects. No compensation or housing alternatives for the residents were provided, ignoring the importance of engaging the local communities.

3.4 Assessing the Damage, Especially in the Housing Sector in an Aim to Determine the Real Need for City

The conflict, destruction, and displacement have induced remarkable change in the urban renewal options in Damascus. The complexity of the situation in Damascus put all the urban policies under the table. There is no clear vision for the future of the reconstruction in Syria. The Syrian civil war has deeply impacted Damascus in two ways: From one side, wide areas of the eastern and southern fringe of Damascus were extensively damaged or destroyed. On the other side, Damascus absorbed the largest shares of the internally displaced persons. As mentioned by a Syrian engineer, in the interview, that "Damascus had 2.4 million people before the conflict, and now we are talking about nearly 3.0 million. So, we are not only talking about massive destruction in buildings and infrastructure but a massive and sudden population increase with the declining economy," which has a great impact on the housing sector of the safer districts. The United Nations Institute for Training and Research (UNITAR) has analyzed and classified the damage density in classes ranging from destroyed, severely damaged, moderately damaged, and undamaged (UNITAR, 2020). According to a UN satellite imagery study on eastern Ghouta, 14% of the assessed buildings in that area were completely destroyed or severely damaged. In 2017, a report released by Save the Children for Ain Tarma town revealed a percentage of 71% of its residential buildings had been destroyed or damaged (Tarrant et al., 2018). As shown in Figs. 3.16 and 3.17.

3.5 The Indirect Urbicide: Zaatari Refugee Camp in Jordan

The crises in Jordan's neighboring countries have contributed to the dramatic increase of the Jordanian population due to the sudden influx of refugees. The current population of Jordan is 10,343,109 as of November 20, 2021, based on Worldometer elaboration of the latest United Nations data (2021). Around 2.9 million non-citizens, including refugees, legal and illegal immigrants from Palestine, Iraq, Syria, and Egypt. In fact, Amman, the capital, has gone through unprecedented growth from 5000 inhabitants to a current estimate of 4 million people within around 100 years (Nilsson & Borges, 2021). The urban sprawl and lack of urban planning in Jordanian cities since the 1960s are highly notable through its infrastructure and services. The significant parts of Jordan's cities have grown parallel with other cities in the MENA region, doubling or tripling because of the regional conflict every 25–30 years (UN-HABITAT, 2021).

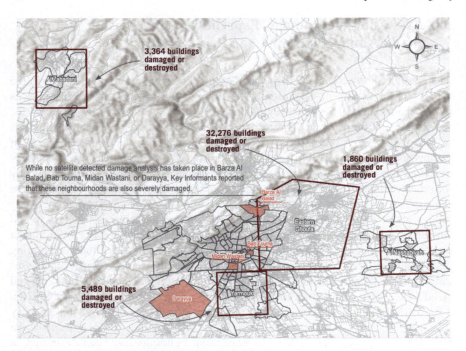

Fig. 3.16 Damascus damage assessment. Ref: UNITAR, 2020

3.5.1 Jordan Urban Scenario: High Level of Urbanization with Poor Planning Strategies

Jordan's cities have grown similar to other cities in the MENA region. Doubling, or depending on regional conflict, tripling every 25–30 years (UN-HABITAT, 2021). Since the 1960s, the Jordanian cities have witnessed a significant urban sprawl led by spontaneous land use planning decisions and some initiatives where the infrastructure is always coming after. For example, the government is obliged to provide road access, electricity, water, and street lighting for any assembly of ten houses (UN-HABITAT, 2021). The hazardous expansion over Jordan's limited natural resources and the lack of coordination between municipalities make the management of this urban expansion a complicated issue. There is a set of laws and regulations that govern building construction and urban planning in Jordan. Municipality law no 29 for 1955 Law of Planning Cities; Towns Villages and Buildings No. 79 for the year 1966 on Planning and building regulations; Jordan National Building Law no. 7/93; Antiquity Law No. 21 for the Year 1988 of Antiquities and Archaeology; Law no. 21/1971—Public Health; Law no. 1 of 2003 Environmental Protection; Agricultural Law No. 20, 1973 and the Amman building and urban planning regulation of 2011 consists of 107 articles regulating the buildings' heights, envelopes, facades, and other general strategies such as architectural extensions, stairways, balconies, and

3.5 The Indirect Urbicide: Zaatari ...   87

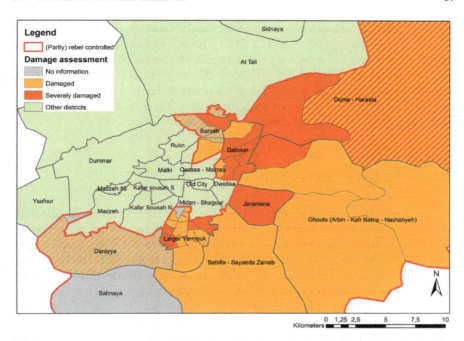

Fig. 3.17 War damage 2011–2018 in districts of Damascus Metropolitan area. Wind & Ibrahim, 2020

site decorations. They organize the land division, parceling, setbacks, and land uses on the planning level. The main urban development regulatory instrument in Jordan is the master plan through Law No. 29/1955, Article 3, which assigns the main responsibilities of the municipal council as outlined in urban planning Article 41/1. The rules governing the planning of towns and streets are designed "to plan the town, open, cancel and change streets, determine their width, and straightness, build them, and construct their sidewalks, and maintain clean, light and name or number them, number the buildings, beautify the town and tree plant it, prevent trespassing, control the streets in terms of what might fall from the open areas, and order their owners to make fences around them." In addition, this article concerns building licenses "to control construction and destruction and changing their forms of and erect electric elevators therein, and give licenses to conduct these works and to specify the location and shape and percentage of the area of the building in proportion to the area of the land on which it is intended to be constructed and to ensure the provision of healthy conditions in it." However, in practice, municipalities do not perform most of the functions assigned to them by law (MOTA, 2005). Despite these laws and regulations, there are several lapses and flaws in the regulatory and legal framework for urban planning. Examples are the absence of a National Urban Policy/ Strategy for Spatial Planning, poor public participation in the planning process, the lack of urban youth zones and the lack of access to information for all and at all levels, and inadequate capacity building and exchange of experiences, knowledge, and expertise in the field of urban planning (UN-HABITA, 2021). Additionally, even though Jordan has always been under different waves of refugees, the Jordanian planning laws and regulations lack an urban policy governing this sudden influx. Consequently, the presence of refugee camps in Jordan shapes a severe and critical spatial phenomenon in which the temporary solutions to host the refugees in camps are transforming into semi-slum zones affecting the urban identity of the Jordanian cities.

3.5.2 Zaatari Refugee Camp

The Zaatari refugee camp is a Syrian refugee camp in the Hashemite Kingdom of Jordan, situated close to the Northern border with Syria, 10 km east of Mafraq (Kimmel, 2014). Within eight years from its institution in 2012, the camp has been gradually transformed from small clusters of tents into a semi-urban settlement. It has grown to become the world's largest Syrian refugee camp (Hyden, 2014) that hosts 76.878 Syrian refugees (UNHCR, 2020). The Zaatari refugee camp has become the symbol of the Syrian displacement across the Middle East. In terms of population, the camp becomes the fourth largest city in Jordan on 25 April 2013, when the camp population reached its peak, and the camp has sheltered 202,993 Syrian refugees (UNHCR, 2020). For the refugees, the camp is the closest destination to their homes and the safest point from the civil war. In an interview with a Syrian refugee who resides in the Zaatari camp, he mentioned that the camp is a temporary haven for the refugees. Still, it lacks sufficient services and appropriate infrastructure that is necessarily required to reconstruct the camp identity as a real functional city. While another female Syrian refugee described life in the camp as a "transitional life." As she felt the transformation of the temporary camp into a more favorable settlement when the tent was replaced with a caravan, when they start having their private bathroom rather than the use of the public one, when they get their own reservoir instead of filling their galloons from the truck water tanks, and finally when she had her own kitchen, as she told us that at the beginning in 2012, every 20 persons shared one kitchen. It's clearly remarkable that despite the refugee camps' intended temporality in planning, politics, and design, they are transforming into a complex urban environment and are developing into a form of housing settlements (Dalal, 2020).

3.5.3 The Population Growth in Zaatari Refugee Camp

The camp population has been dramatically elevated since its institution in July 2012, see the expansion of the camp in Fig. 3.18, as it emerged as the largest population center in the Mafraq governorate within a few months (Oxfam, 2020).

3.5 The Indirect Urbicide: Zaatari … 89

Fig. 3.18 Zaatari refugee camp. Ref: BBC, 2016

After the first month of the camp opening, precisely according to UNHCR statistics on 27 August 2012, the camp population was 15,000 refugees, inhabiting 10% of the total number of Syrian refugees in Jordan. The camp population has been tripled, to be 45,000, within less than six months (UNHCR, 2020). The notable jump was in April 2013 when the camp housed more than 200,000 refugees, as shown in Fig. 3.19. Gradually, the camp population decreased when some of the refugees decided to leave the camp for other new instituted camps or seek refuge in other countries and few of them returned to their homeland as a lawyer interviewee told us in our interview with him, that the return from Zaatari was not obvious between refugees. He mentioned that the Naseeb crossing border between Jordan and Syria was reopened on 15 October 2018; from that date until this moment, the number of returnees didn't exceed 35,000, although the Syrian regime is actively and repeatedly calling for the return of the Syrian refugees, especially those in Jordan. Still, the vast majority don't have the courage to return.

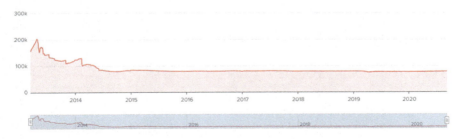

Fig. 3.19 Zaatari camp population growth from 2012–2020. Ref: UNHCR, 2020

Consequently, this sudden change in the camp population, which is hardly expectable, requires strong planning that able to manage the refugees' demands over the urban environment. The growth rate in Zaatari camp was faster than any normal city. It is linked to two main factors: the first one is the natural growth rate in which the total number of births in Zaatari since its institution is around 10,000 (Alabaster, 2016). The second factor is the continuous decampments for the Syrian, as, at the beginning of the Syrian civil war, the camp received 1500 Syrian refugees every night (UNHCR, 2020). The Syrian refugees' influx to Zaatari camp was shortly beyond the camp capacity envisioned before. The fluctuated population played a significant role in modifying the camp design capacity and formed critical difficulties in the camp planning regarding the users' ratios (Helm et al., 2017).

3.5.4 The Zaatari Camp, Urban Housing, and Spatial Planning: The Abrupt Space for Emergency

The distinction between housing, camp, and the city is gradually collapsing in contemporary humanitarianism of the twentieth century. Contemporary refugee spaces provide housing for the refugees in camps and connect them to urban labor market all at the same time (Herscher, 2017) (Fig. 3.20).

The Zaatari camp planning was very experimental. In terms of the camp's spatial evolution, its infrastructure's expansion, the increased population, and the structures' transformation (Dalal, 2020). The Zaatari camp master plan revealed a grid system planning in which the camp skeleton was defined through blocks and streets. The Zaatari camp has been defined as a city in the perspective of different scholars. For example, it is referred to as "the Syrian city in exile" by Al-Makhdhi (2014), "the instant city" by Smith (2014), "the makeshift city" by Dorai (2016), and "the temporary city" by Alshoubaki and Zazzara (2018). The camp has been divided by

Fig. 3.20 Zaatari refugee camp. Ref: WFP, 2013

3.5 The Indirect Urbicide: Zaatari …

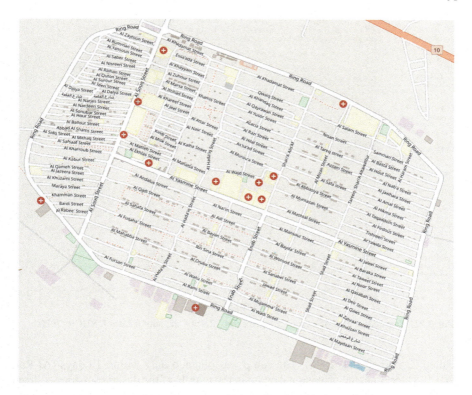

Fig. 3.21 Street networks in Zaatari refugee camo. Ref: OpenStreetMap, 2020

two main streets, Market street and Yasmeen Street, with a ring road of 8.3 km that encircles the whole camp, and 122 alleys running through the camp. As shown in Fig. 3.21.

The most popular street in the camp is Al-Souq street or known in the camp as Cham Élysées, which includes a great number of shops, food stalls, small restaurants, pastries, and supermarkets.

The camp planning and its public facilities are in the middle zone between the formal camp identity that reflects the bare life conditions, or the informal one, reflecting the refugees' power in structuring their spaces (Katz, 2017). The spatial arrangement in the Zaatari refugee camp reflects the rigorous impact of the standards drawn by the actors in charge (Dalal, 2020). According to UNHCR (2020), the camp, which has an area of 5.3 km^2, includes more than 26,000 prefabricated shelters, and each of them has its own private kitchen and latrine.

The camp settlement area has 32 schools, 58 community centers, 2 hospitals, 9 healthcare centers, and 1 delivery unit. See the camp master plan shown in Fig. 3.22.

During the first half of the camp establishment year, the satellite images showed extemporaneous planning, in which rows of tents were arranged near a small village

Fig. 3.22 The master plan of Zaatari refugee camp. Ref: by the author from UNHCR, 2020

called Zaatari (Dalal, 2020). The camp was planned only within 19 days (Al-Rai, 2012). Over time, the provisional camp in the middle of the desert transformed from a bare land into a semi-structured city. The camp was planned based on the United Nations Higher Commissioner for Refugees, UNHCR, planning standards which determined a 3.5 m^2 covered living area per person in which one family of 4–6 persons live in one residential unit; they allocate 45 m^2 of camp size per person, they assign 1 school to serve a population of 5000 persons, one health center and one market place to for 20,000 persons (UNHCR, 2020). Scholars showed that the existing planning standards are not enough. Still, instead, they will shape extra risk with time, and as soon as the refugees start expanding outside the limited space given initially to them (Kennedy, 2004, 2005, 2008; Herz, 2008; Alshoubaki & Zazzara, 2020). These risks include economic, social, political, environmental, and health risks. In fact, because of the crowded spaces and the lack of infrastructure, refugee camps are often unhygienic, driving a high incidence of infectious diseases and epidemics (Unite for sight, 2021). As well, Large camps with a high density cause significant environmental damage because the refugees use and pollute water, deplete wood supplies for fuel, and poach animals for food, often harming parks, nature reserves, and World Heritage Sites. These impacts make host countries less willing to receive more refugees (Hammer & Ahmed, 2021). Another risk is connecting to the temporary materials and the poor conditions of the temporary shelters that used in camp design which is the fire hazards as it was reported by the BBC (2011) that the shelters provided to tsunami victims had poor fire resistance that led to the loss of their lives. The impact of the camp planning strategies and standards have their short-term and long-term ramification on the city urban fabric.

3.6 Conclusion

Violence in cities could be direct or indirect, as discussed in this chapter. The direct urbicide in Damascus city in Syria and the indirect urbicide in Zaatari camp in Jordan. From one side, it was essential to analyze and address Damascus's spatial and urban development and transformation over history, which unfolds multiple historical metamorphoses to achieve an integrated spatial planning policy capable of regenerating a city with urban identity. Analyzing the urban scenery of post-conflict Damascus and the Syrian approach in construction by studying and investigating the land tenure, the spatial planning laws, and the reconstruction decrees proved that the current and previous rules of redevelopment and construction in Syria have different gaps in terms of the project's scale, scope, and timeline. In fact, there is a lack of a comprehensive nationwide program that specifies a set of guidelines for the redevelopment, which encompasses different stakeholders and links large geographical areas. The construction laws lack a specific timetable that determines the total time required for any project from planning to execution. Notably, they lack a comprehensive strategic plan that fulfills the community's needs, desires, goals, and aspirations, as noticed in the redevelopment projects. No compensation or housing alternatives for the residents were provided, ignoring the importance of engaging the local communities.

From the other side, it was crucial to shed light on the "indirect urbicide" which was termed by this research, within the context of Zaatari refugee camp, by analyzing the camp context, assessing the Syrian refugees' needs, and monitoring the risk in housing, infrastructure, and spatial planning. The sudden change in the camp population, which is hardly expectable, requires vital planning to manage the refugees' demands over the urban environment since the growth rate in Zaatari camp was faster than in any normal city. The Zaatari camp planning has been very experimental. In terms of the camp's spatial evolution, its infrastructure's expansion, the increased population, and the structures' transformation. The camp planning situation is hanging between the temporary and the permanent status shaping informal zones with no identity reflecting only the impact of the transformation of the camp standards drawn by the actors in charge.

References

Abdulac, S. (1982). Damas: Les années Ecochard (1932–1982). *Cahiers De La Recherche Architecturale, No, 11*, 32–44.
Akram, A. I. (2004). The sword of allah: Khalid bin al-waleed—His life and campaigns, Oxford University Press. ISBN 0-19-597714-9

Al-Makhadhi, S. (2014). Zaatari: The Syrian city in exile. Delayed Gratification. Retrieved from https://www.slow-journalism.com/from-the-archive/zaatari-the-syrian-city-in-exile

Alabaster, O. (2016). Syrian refugees mark 5,000th birth at Zaatari Clinic. Refugees News|Al Jazeera. Retrieved from https://www.aljazeera.com/news/2016/3/2/syrian-refugees-mark-5000th-birth-at-zaatari-clinic

Alshoubaki, H., & Zazzara, L. (2020). The fragility in the land of refugees: Jordan and irrepressible phenomenon of refugee camps. *Journal of International Studies, 13*(1), 123–142. https://doi.org/10.14254/2071-8330.2020/13-1/8

Arfeh, H. (2016). The institutionalization of demographic change in Syria. Retrieved, 2020, from https://www.atlanticcouncil.org/blogs/syriasource/the-institutionalization-of-demographic-change-in-syria/

Arnaud, J. L. (2006) Damas: Urbanisme et Architecture, 1860–1925 Paris: Sinbad-Actes Sud

Bauman, Z., 2019. The century of camps. In: P. Beilharz (Ed.), *The Bauman reader* (pp. 230). Oxford: Wiley.

BBC. (2011, March 12). Japan earthquake: Struggle to reach tsunami survivors. BBC News. Retrieved from https://www.bbc.com/news/world-asia-pacific-12721977

Bianca, S. (2000) Urban form in the Arab World: Past and present London: Thames & Hudson.

Bonine, M. E. (1977). From uruk to casablanca: Perspectives on the urban experience of the middle east. *Journal of Urban History, 3*(2), 141–180.

Burns, R. (2005). Damascus: A history. Routledge & amp; CRC Press. Retrieved from https://www.routledge.com/Damascus-A-History/Burns/p/book/9781138483354

Calamur, K. (March 15, 2019)."No One Wants to Help Bashar al-Assad Rebuild Syria". Atlantic. Atlantic. Archived from the original on 3 August 2019. Retrieved 2020

Centre, U. N. E. S. C. O. W. H. (2019). Ancient city of Damascus. UNESCO World Heritage Centre. Retrieved from https://whc.unesco.org/en/list/20/.

Daher, J. (2019). The paradox of Syria's reconstruction. Carnegie Middle East Center. Retrieved from https://carnegie-mec.org/2019/09/04/paradox-of-syria-s-reconstruction-pub-79773.

Dalal, A. (2020). The refugee camp as urban housing. *Housing Studies*. https://doi.org/10.1080/02673037.2020.1782850

Doraï, M. K. (2010) Palestinian refugee camps in Lebanon: Migration, mobility and the urbanization process. In A. Knudsen and S. Hanafi (eds.), *Palestinian refugees: Identity, space and place in the Levant*, Routledge, Abingdon.

Eldredge, N., & Horenstein S. (2014). Concrete jungle: New York City and our last best hope for a sustainable future (pp. 21). University of California Press. ISBN 978–0–520–27015–2.

Elfeituri, N. (2021) The "Solidere" effect and the localisation of heritage reconstruction in post-war transitions, Libya. In F. F. Arefian, J. Ryser, A. Hopkins, & J. Mackee (Eds.), Historic cities in the face of disasters. The urban book series. Springer. https://doi.org/10.1007/978-3-030-77356-4_17

ETH. (2012, August 10). The Urban Development of Syria. Retrieved December 2020, from https://press.uchicago.edu/ucp/books/author/B/E/au25046652.html

Fawaz, L. (1994). An occasion for war—Civil conflict in lebanon and Damascus in 1860. University of California Press. p. 139. ISBN 0–520–08782–8.

Fries, F. (1994) 'Les Plans d'Alep et de Damas, un Banc d'Essai pour l'Urbanisme des Frères Danger 1931–1937 "Figures de l'Orientalisme en Architecture" Revue de Monde Musulman et de la Mediteranee No 73–74 Aix en Provence: Edisur (pp. 311–326).

Fries, F. (2000) Damas (1860–1946) La mise en place de la ville moderne. PhD thesis University of Paris 8

Hamedi, S. (2018, May 12). Minister of housing to Al-Watan: Amending the expropriation law is not proposed and Laws 66, 10 and 23 solve housing problems. Retrieved May, 2020, from https://alwatan.sy/archives/150723

References

Hammer, L., & Ahmed, S. (2021, June 2). Refugee camps can wreak enormous environmental damages—Should source countries be liable for them? The Conversation. Retrieved from https://theconversation.com/refugee-camps-can-wreak-enormous-environmental-damages-should-source-countries-be-liable-for-them-152519

Hanna, E., & Harastani, N. (2019). Is marota city the type of reconstruction syrians need? Retrieved 2020, from: www.thealeppoproject.com/wp-content/uploads/2019/05/Is-Marota-City-the-Reconstruction-Syrians-Need.pdf

Hanna. (2018). The politics of urban reconstruction in Syria. Retrieved April, 2020, from https://blogs.ucl.ac.uk/dpublog/2018/07/02/politics-urban-reconstruction-syria/

Herscher, A. (2017) Critical spatial practice 9: Displacement architecture and refugee. In N. Hirsch & M. Miessen (Eds.), Sternberg Press.

Herz, M. (ed.). (2013). *From camp to city: Refugee camps of the Western Sahara*. Lars Müller.

Hopwood, D. (1988) *Syria 1945–1986: Politics and society*. Routledge.

Howard J. (2019). "The Syrian Civil War Is Coming to an End". rand. RAND Corporation. Archived from the original on 20 July 2019. Retrieved 2020.

Jbour, S. (2002). The reality of the informal settlements in Syria. Retrieved 2020, from https://wsfb.files.wordpress.com

JEA. (2018). Amman building and urban planning regulation of 2011. Jordanian Engineers Association. Retrieved from https://www.jea.org.jo/portal/en/amman-building-urban-planning-regulation-of-2011/.

Kallaa, M. A. (1993) Les Temps de l'Urbanisme: Enquêtes d'Histoire Orale: Damas et le Temps d'Ecochard PhD Thesis Paris: University VIII.

Katz, I. (2015). Spreading and concentrating: The camp as the space of the frontier. *City, 19*(5), 727–740.

Katz, I. (2017). "Between bare life and everyday life: Spatialising Europe's migrant camps. *Amps: Architecture_Media_Politics_Society (UCL Press)*.

Kennedy, J. (2008). Structures for the displaced: Service and identity in refugee settlements. Delft: International Forum of Urbanism.

Kimmelman, M. (2014, July 05). Refugee camp for Syrians in Jordan evolves as a do-it-yourself city. Retrieved December 04, 2020, from https://www.nytimes.com/2014/07/05/world/middleeast/zaatari-refugee-camp-in-jordan-evolves-as-a-do-it-yourself-city.html

Lababedi, Z. (2008). The urban development of Damascus : A study of its past , present and future. *UCL Discovery, London*, 73. Retrieved from http://discovery.ucl.ac.uk/14328/1/14328.pdf.

Ma'oz, M. (1968) *Ottoman reform in Syria and Palestine, 1840–1861: The impact of the tanzima*. Clarendon Press.

Mansour, H. (2016). The lost identity of the city: The case of Damascus. Retrieved from https://www.researchgate.net/publication/286252741_The_lost_identity_of_the_city_The_case_of_Damascus.

MOTA. (2005). Legal framework-suggested best practices. Retrieved from https://mota.gov.jo/ebv4.0/root_storage/ar/eb_list_page.

Myers, D. P. (1922). Source Mmaterial. *The Journal of International Relations, 12*(3), 436–445.

Nasr, J. (2018). Assad's property law hits hope of return for Syrians in Germany. Reuters retrieved from https://www.reuters.com/article/uk-mideast-crisis-syria-germany-insight-idUKKBN1JA1V4.

Nilsson, K., & Borges, L. (2021, August 2). Amman, one of the fastest grown cities in the world, is moving towards sustainable city planning. Nordregio. Retrieved from https://nordregio.org/amman-one-of-the-fastest-grown-cities-in-the-world-is-moving-towards-sustainable-city-planning/.

Njoh, A. J. (2016) Rationale for french colonial urbanism. In *French urbanism in foreign lands*. Springer. https://doi.org/10.1007/978-3-319-25298-8_1

OHCHR. (207AD). HLP rights, migration and business activity in Syria - OHCHR. Retrieved from https://www.ohchr.org/Documents/Issues/Business/2019Survey/OtherStakeholders/SDLP3.pdf

OXFAM. (2020). Life in Za'atari, the largest Syrian refugee camp in the world. Retrieved October, 2020, from https://www.oxfam.org/en/life-zaatari-largest-syrian-refugee-camp-world.

Smith, D. (2014). SomaLia: Refugee camp brings solar energy into computer classrooms. Retrieved 2020, from https://womennewsnetwork.net/2013/08/12/somalia-refugee-camp-solar-computer

Tarrant, R., Corbett, E., & Grogan, P. (2018). Mapping the destruction of damascus in the syrian conflict. Retrieved December 09, 2020, from https://storyful.com/resources/blog/how-war-has-changed-syrias-landscape-mapping-the-destruction-of-east-damascus/

UN-HABITAT. (2021). Jordan—urban issues: UN-HABITAT. UN. Retrieved from https://unhabitat.org/jordan-urban-issues.

UNHCR. (2020). Zaatari refugee camp—factsheet, July 2020—Jordan. Retrieved, 2020, from https://reliefweb.int/report/jordan/zaatari-refugee-camp-factsheet-july-2020

UNITAR-UNOSAT. (2015), Four years of human suffering—The Syria conflict as observed through satellite imagery,

UNITAR. (2020). Syria world heritage sites report. Retrieved, 2020, from https://unitar.org/sustainable-development-goals/satellite-analysis-and-applied-research/chs-syria

Unite for sight. Healthcare in Refugee Camps and Settlements. (2021). Retrieved from http://www.uniteforsight.org/refugee-health/module1.

Weber, S. (2002) 'Damascus: A major Eastern Mediterranean site at risk' ICOMOS www.international.icomos.org/risk/2001/syri2001.htm

Wifstrand, E., & J. Ria (2009) Modern Damascus.

Wind, B., & Ibrahim, B. (2020, January 14). The war-time urban development of Damascus: How the geography-and political economy of warfare affects housing patterns. Retrieved October 04, 2020, from https://www.sciencedirect.com/science/article/pii/S0197397519309464

Worldmeter. (2021). Jordan population (live). Worldometer. Retrieved from https://www.worldometers.info/world-population/jordan-population/.

Yassar, K., & Kafa, M. (2009). Discussion of random and informal settlements in Damascus. *Geo-spatial Information Science, 12* (4), 289–295. https://doi.org/10.1007/s11806-009-0100-9

Zazzara, L., & Alshoubaki, H. (2018). *Reconstructing cities in peacetime: Urban issues in post-war scenarios.* Carsa edizioni.

Chapter 4
Urban Emergency Integrated Planning UEIP

Abstract This chapter discusses and synthesizes the two selected case studies, Damascus city and Zaatari refugee camp, within three main spheres: the spatial sphere, the diagnostic and assessment sphere, and the construction laws and the technical standards sphere. The case studies proved firstly the absence of a wide-ranging theory in spatial planning that covers post-conflict situations for providing temporary living environments. Secondly, the inadequacy of the current implemented planning strategies to meet the reconstruction challenges in post-war cases. Thirdly, the time factor has permanently been excluded from planning policies. This chapter proposes an innovative conceptual framework to confront these gaps: Urban Emergency Integrated Planning—[UEIP]. UEIP emerged to handle the post-conflict displacement resulting from the Syrian civil war by discussing the urban politics necessary to provide fully functional cities for two types of war victims: refugees in host countries and returnees to their homelands.

Keywords Spatial sphere · Diagnostic sphere · Construction laws · UEIP

The mass flow of the Syrian refugees to the surrounding countries, especially to Jordan, Lebanon, or Europe, produced a decline in the Syrian republic's total population. In contrast, the population of the capital, Damascus, has been perilously increased because of the internally displaced persons who fled from the conflicted zones to the capital.

Consequently, the sudden population influx to cities, who are in urgent need of housing as a result of displacement, is a critical issue that doesn't require a single development project but adaptable spatial planning that able to deal with the sudden urgent need for housing, as well as capable of understanding the current urban environment which is full of uncertainties and complexities that does not have enough time to deal with.

The analyses focused on Syrian displaced population issue in the two cases, the Syrian refugees in Jordan who were accommodated in the Zaatari refugee camp, and the returnees to their homeland, specifically Damascus, who are in urgent need of housing in totally or partially destroyed zones. For both cases, the role of integrated spatial planning in building sustainable urban housing in post-conflict situations has been analyzed within three main spheres:

- the spatial sphere;
- the diagnostic and assessment sphere; and
- the construction laws and the technical standards sphere.

The phenomenon under investigation is a multilayer interlaced issue where three main factors govern the territory transformation: the space, the risk, and the law. The three-spheres therefore outlie the analytic strategy to cover all factors. This complex situation requires analyzing the space in its current spatial situation, assessing the existing threats and challenges, and then evaluating the efficiency of the current laws and standards that govern the construction and reconstruction for the two cases under investigation.

4.1 The Spatial Sphere

As Clerc (2014, P.2) clarifies, "Conflicts are indeed exceptional times when the bones of the territorial political and economic strategic dimensions of urban planning are laid bare.......... at the expense of spatial and design considerations." The spatial sphere discusses the impact of spatial planning and the urban development on dealing with the urgent need for housing on the Damascus city in Syria and the Zaatari refugee camp in Jordan. The spatial sphere indicated that any new city proposal, even in emergencies, should be connected to the existing urban fabric. Evidently, the spatial analysis of Damascus and its urban development demonstrates two scenarios for the population need for housing during the reconstruction process: The first scenario recognizes the areas out of Damascus master plan, specifically, the slums and informal settlements such as the Rural Damascus. The second scenario concerns the Syrian cities that are completely destroyed, especially in Damascus's peripheral areas, such as Darya.

The complexity of spatial reality and urban development affects any reconstruction project. One of the most complicated issues regarding the returnees' rehousing and Damascus reconstruction is the development of the informal settlements within Damascus spatial pattern. According to the Syrian Ministry of Housing (2007), between 30 and 40% of housing within the Syrian cities is informal housing. As highlighted by an interviewee—a Syrian civil engineer, the intricacy of the informal housing issue in Syria is linked to the ownership registers which aren't adequately mirrored in the real estate registry and to the land division regulations that in turn aggravated Damascus's spatial scenario. As before the Syrian Civil War, it was compulsory to divide the land plots with a minimum of 4000 m^2, but in fact, people live within an area of 100 m^2 or less. Consequently, before the Syrian Civil War, the regulations only governed and organized large-scale plots. In reality, more than 40 properties within the same plot are out of regulations; in other words, the small-scale properties are out of the organizational measures; thus, they form random neighborhoods. By the same token, after the Syrian Civil War, the damage in these informal settlements was extensive. For instance, what happened in Eastern Ghouta after the

4.1 The Spatial Sphere

five-year battle (2013–2018) has devastated whole neighborhoods (OHCHR, 2018). The UN satellite imagery analysis reported that 93% of buildings had been damaged or destroyed in one district of Ghouta (Rodgers et al., 2018). As stated by another Syrian expert in construction field that one missile collided in the unplanned zone produced more harm and damage than 10 missiles in an organized area because of the absence of the spacing distance "buildings setbacks" in the slum areas and their poor structure skeleton which does not bear the attacks.

The spatial analysis showed that the situation in Damascus city stands within two prospects: the first is regarding the slum areas that are not subject to regulation, such as rural Damascus, East Damascus, Southeast Damascus, the eastern Ghouta, and the extension of Kafr Sousa where the urban structure of these zones is not much complicated as told by a Syrian planner.

The second involves Damascus peripheral zones where they were originally part of the Damascus master plan and are now totally damaged or destroyed, such as Darya and Harasta. 70% of Damascus peripheries were destroyed. The analysis showed that Damascus's current spatial pattern and urban development lack appropriate city planning strategies and urban design tools; it also proves the absence of housing typologies and the residential compounds in any project.

As discussed by an interviewee—a Syrian expert in spatial planning, Syria witnessed a kind of modernization and development only during 2005 as it appeared in the Qudussiyah suburb and Dumar suburb or known as the Dumar project "Mashro'o Dumar" in Al-Safarat neighborhood on Damascus outskirts. Still, some of the construction redevelopment projects are underway, and these redevelopment projects were out of reach of the major part of the Syrian society. Another interviewee—an expert in the construction field—stated that a redevelopment project known as Marota city is out of reach of 90–95% of the Syrian population. It is only affordable for the rich, the top 5–10% group of income and wealth distribution.

The Syrian Civil War has contributed to creating a notable change in the demographic distribution of the Syrian population as noted in the spatial analysis and reinforced by a Syrian researcher that pre-war Syria had a good demographic distribution within the city scale and the governorate scale. Still, with the beginning of the Syrian Civil War, the population pressure concentrated on the governorates' capitals because they were the safest.

In fact, Damascus city's organizational plan does not commensurate with the damage degree or the war ramifications. As an interviewee—a Syrian planner stated "It is impossible to reconstruct a city after passing a horrible war by using a land use master plan that only allocates the percentage of industrial, commercial, residential, and agricultural land". In summary, a plan doesn't correspond with what the war left, starting from the consequences of the demographic change in the Syrian population composition.

In parallel, the spatial scenery of the Zaatari refugee camp shows its transformation into a semi-structured city since its institution in 2012. As a Syrian refugee who has lived in the camp since 2013 stated, "the camp is my safe temporary home; I have basic ingredients for a decent life, but they have a very provisional character". According to him, refugees have resilience and evident willingness to live, survive, and continue and for these reasons, the camp started to have a permanent character. In fact, the camp doesn't grow only in numbers and its habitable area but also is solidifying. Another interviewee—a Syrian refugee woman who has lived in the camp since 2012—argued that "we don't mind about what they gave us a tent or caravan, we construct, in every possible way, what we can live in."

There are several complexities and contradictions between the spatial sphere and the need for sustainable urban resettlement in a post-conflict situation. In both two cases, the territory faced massive and sudden mass influx within a short time. Consequently, there emerged critical tensions between the temporary solutions and the existing spatial patterns. The rigid temporary housing techniques form zones of informalities odds with the existing urban fabric. The contradictions in the implemented emergency housing are two-fold. One is between the spatial plan and the actual development of the settlement and transformation seen in the Zaatari camp. The Zaatari camp's spatial plan was drawn based on the humanitarian standards to give it a temporal look. Still, in fact, it is in a state of continuous transformation toward the permanent character. The collection of shelters is gradually transformed into a semi-functional city. Another contradiction concerns the time factor, which also plays a vital role in transforming these temporary structures into decaying cities, shaping an arbitrary expansion over the territory. Although housing in emergencies requires quick responses, it also requires a context-specified response. An emergency housing project must address both to integrate with the city's urban scenery continuously. Refugee camps are designed as a prompt response to lodging the refugees for a short-time period. Still, the refugees reside in these camps for years, as seen in the Zaatari camp, which has been instituted as a solution for a few months. However, since 2012, the camp has been standing still with more than 79,000 refugees (UNHCR, 2021). As stated by Kleinschmidt one of the world's leading authorities on humanitarian aid, "These are the cities of tomorrow." (Radford, 2016). According to the UNHCR report (2004), the average stay in camps is 17 years; that's a whole generation.

4.2 Diagnostic Sphere

The diagnostic sphere as a practical appraisal tool helped in assessing the situation and the challenges that face resettlement issues for the refugees and returnees in post-conflict situations of the Damascus city and Zaatari refugee camp. It aimed to assess the fundamental challenges that impact the formation of a functional urban settlement in both cases.

The urban diagnostic approach, as mentioned by Leach et al. (2019), helps planners and policymakers create a grounded set of evidence-based interventions that parallel with a set of city performance measures compared to the city performance in the future. It was quite essential to discuss and analyze the urban challenges of the two cases to understand the direct urbicide and the indirect urbicide phenomena within a grounded context with an aim to propose the appropriate urban policy that corresponds with the reality.

4.2 Diagnostic Sphere

From the one side, in Damascus, there are many complexities and overlapping challenges; political, economic, social, organizational, and financial that impact the resettlement and the housing issue of the returnees. As discussed by an interviewee—an expert in the spatial development field in Syria, besides the absence of disaster management strategies in Syria, there are political, economic, social, organizational, and financial factors that made the actions toward managing the post-war state very chaotic. The required funds for a comprehensive reconstruction plan in Syria are improbable to happen because of the attitude of the Syrian leadership, the economic implications of the Covid-19 pandemic, and the geopolitical interests of regional and global powers and the sources (Wissenschaft, 2020). By the same token, another interviewee—a Syrian expert in field of environmental engineering—confirmed that the opposed sanctions from the international committees on the Syrian government create a spoke in the reconstruction wheel and on the application of the national reconstruction plans and initiatives. In this manner, another expert interviewee also said a robust reconstruction requires sufficient financial aids from the World Bank, the Arab League, and the Islamic Support Council. She also stressed the need to reframe the urban policies and the local government's reconstruction laws to conform with the war ramifications on the Damascus territorial structure.

Another critical challenge is the social dimension, which has been extensively hit by the Syrian Civil War. A prominent evidence is that the conflict has sharpened the religious segregation. As interviewees expressed, the pre-war Damascus had no sectarian distinction between Shiite and Sunni or Muslims and Christians. Damascus was a mix of ethnic groups within the same neighborhood. Diversity and ethnicity were overrepresented in several neighborhoods in Damascus, such as Assyrians, Eastern Orthodox Christians, Shiite, Sunni, Alawites, Druz, or Kurds (Fuccaro, 2003; Naito, 1988). Before the Syrian Civil War, they shaped specific patterns and a particular approach to planning and housing designs. Thus, the post-war disintegration in social and sectoral strata will be an essential challenge in the reconstruction process and in reorganizing Damascus city and its spatial and social components. The reason is that Syrian people from diverse sects have lost their confidence in each other and in this social dimension will impact the rehousing process. In this way, the provision of housing alternatives and site selection for settlements since the conflict has been transformed into a sectarian war that negatively affects the society's social components and social structure and thus the relationship between the inhabitants. The warfare has negatively impacted the social contract of the Syrian society and the community's relationships because of the religious sects, ethnic, socioeconomic, and sociopolitical segregation. Therefore, the social dimension should be highly considered by the spatial planners to outline new urban policies that address the social structure imbalance.

After diagnosing the main challenges that impact the resettlement process for the returnees to Damascus city and after evaluating the current conditions within a micro-level, we found that the challenges range from the local scale to the global one within different dimensions: economic, financial, legal, social, institutional, spatial, organizational, and governmental that govern the reconstruction process and regulate the returnees' urgent need for housing and require a comprehensive integrated planning approach capable of building a sustainable urban resettlement in such situations.

For the other case, diagnosing the Zaatari refugee camp metamorphosis indicated that the refugee camp has been spatially and structurally transformed into a semi-functional city after around 8 years of its institution. However, these spaces will never dissolve into vapor but rather they are solidifying within their underdeveloped conditions. While Zaatari refugee camp provides average facilities that protect the refugees and provide them with the minimum living conditions, this marginal living has a deep impact on the camp spatial metamorphosis. The camp residents seek to improve their current living spaces based on their needs and aspirations, which are highly developed with time. Yet the required developments and improvements are not controlled or regulated; they are rather chaotic and hazardous. As a result, these spaces remodeled into permanent anarchic urban zones in the camp, which is sprawling over Al-Mafraq desert as illustrated in Fig. 4.1.

The hazardous quick transformation of the Zaatari refugee camp shapes a real challenge. The Zaatari camp that has been established within 9 days is now a bustling home to around 80,000 Syrian refugees (UNHCR, 2015a, 2015b), tents were replaced with prefabricated caravans, refugees started making their own interventions that shaped a *city-like* camp. As Lazareva (2016) mentioned, the Syrian refugees came for 15 days, but many more years passed, and they still live there. It now has 26,000

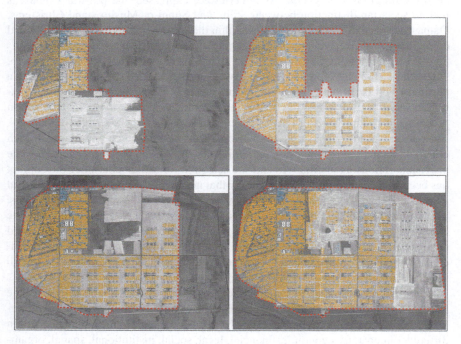

Fig. 4.1 The evolution of Zaatari refugee camp in one year from November 15.2012–February 26.2013. Ref: UNITAR-UNOSAT, 2013

prefabricated shelters that lodge almost 80,000 Syrian refugees with 32 schools, eight medical clinics, 58 community centers (UNHCR, 2021).

In order to diagnose the current situation in the camp, it was imperative to conduct meetings and to ask the camp resident refugees themselves about the challenges, obstacles, and threats that they endure within the camp settlement. Obviously, Zaatari residents face social, organizational, spatial, and institutional inconveniences. They suffer from poor infrastructure and the very poor street networks prohibiting them from moving across the camp smoothly. Interviewees stated that the camp residents endure serious problems because of the improper road network conditions. Firstly, the bumpy roads hindered the ambulances and the emergency vehicles from doing their work smoothly. Secondly, the muddy paths obstruct those who roam within the camp districts on foot or by bikes, especially in winter and rainy seasons, because the roads are slippery, dirty, and dangerous. Thirdly, the dusty roads in the dry seasons especially in summer create breathing and respiratory problems for residents when the strong winds flow. Fourthly, the improper street networks prevent the people with disabilities from practicing their life normally, apparently, disabled persons' needs are out of the camp planning standards and emergency managers' concern. Disabled persons can't leave their caravans since nothing planned in a way that serve them.

Another issue is that the camp lacks greenery which influences the refugees' health and well-being. An interviewee—a refugee who has lived in the camp since 2013—put it in words as "we are depressed and we need to see green color, our eyes get sick of this vast area of bright white caravans in the mid of this bare desert."

The analysis shows that the new camp developments are still built with a semi-temporary character until now (as of autumn 2021) despite the fact that the camp has becoming less and less "a temporary solution." The residents are allowed to transform their spaces only using temporary materials such as aluminum sheets and pieces of cloth. Consequently, the refugees start using different temporary materials for expanding their residential units, which don't relate to their construction culture. An interviewee—a Syrian housewife from Dara'a who has resided in Zaatari since 2014—told that "we are losing our identity in this temporary safe place."

The camp develops by time another kind of risks such as fires, because of the used material in constructing the camp which are not fire resistant and because of the size of the residential units.

Another interviewee—a Syrian refugee—said that "the camp gives us protection from missiles, but we are not secure from other threats."

In fact, caravans protect refugees from explosions but not from desertic and harsh weather conditions, intolerable heat and frigid temperature, heavy rainfall, and the danger of insects, snakes, and other predators. This is not easy to child refugees neither. As an interviewee—a Syrian child refugee—pointed out, "the caravan is not my home. My home in Syria was warm, but here, I can't sleep on rainy nights because the water leaks into the caravan unit." As a result, and in attempts to make their living environment more tolerable, refugees modify their settlements based on their urgent need to appropriate safety and comfortable space with some level of privacy.

As mentioned by another interviewee—a Syrian woman who has lived in the camp since 2014, "at the beginning, we thought that the tent would be enough because we will return soon, but here we are after six years in the same place. By the time we found that we needed spaces that maintain our privacy. In fact, neither the tent nor the caravan provides that." Obviously, poor living conditions inside Zaatari refugee camp, lack of access to clean water, inadequate water supplies and sanitation, poor housing and home conditions, bad personal hygiene, crowded spaces, hot surfaces, and material have shaped the urban scenery of Zaatari refugee camp.

The hazardous transformation in Zaatari is linked to different reasons; firstly, Governments and humanitarian agencies tend to implement a simple design and easy and quick planning to accommodate refugees. Consequently, they implement grid patterns to accommodate the maximum number of refugees in a small piece of land granted by the host country. That creates different environmental health problems and diseases because of the limited spaces and setbacks between tents. A strategy that does not consider space transformation in the long run.

The camp transformed into a more chaotic space since its opening in July 2012, Zaatari witnessed a dramatic increase in its population, making it the largest population center in Mafraq Governorate within a few months (UNHCR, 2014). This tremendous acceleration in population creates dense spaces with no identity, as a Syrian refugee interviewee clarified this: "I can't call home, camp, or settlement. It is, in fact, a refugees' storage."

Secondly; the absence of appropriate strategies that govern the improvements produced by the refugees themselves. Consequently, the modifications lack support, organization, and coordination between refugees and experts in construction and spatial planning.

4.3 Construction Laws and the Technical Standards Sphere

Construction and reconstruction are processes that have been always governed by laws and legislations. Consequently, this sphere studies the situation of the current construction laws in both cases under investigation. As noticed, in the case of Damascus, the discussion of this sphere concerns the current planning laws and the reconstruction regulations that will impact the process of reconstructing Damascus after the Syrian Civil war. Meanwhile, the analysis of the Zaatari camp focuses on the technical planning standards used in planning refugee camps.

The current sphere discusses Damascus spatial planning laws, the land tenure, and the latest construction decrees such as law 10, law No.33, and law 9. As argued by an expert professional interviewee, the Syrians are not only victims of the civil war, but they are victims of iniquitous laws, especially law 10 and decree 66 because these laws in practice are doing something utterly different than a reconstruction plan as they neglect the social dimension, and for this reason, they must be abolished. Importantly, the current and previous construction laws and redevelopment regulations in Syria lack a comprehensive nationwide strategy that manages and coordinates the spatial planning process, determines the project's scale, defines its scope and timeline, and specifies stakeholders and links large geographical areas. As discussed previously

4.3 Construction Laws and the Technical Standards Sphere

about the Law 10, of Housing, Land, and Property allow the Syrian government to assign any area in Syria for redevelopment. Then, authorities have one week to request a list of property owners from local real estate authorities and existing land registries (Tahrir, 2019). Consequently, this law mentions the local population just for the proof of ownership, but they don't have any active participation in the redevelopment process. Moreover, this law is unfair in the allotted time to prove ownership. The Norwegian Refugee Council found that only 17% of displaced Syrians say they have paperwork proving ownership of their property in Syria. This lack of documents makes it difficult, if not impossible, to reclaim property (Al-Jablawi, 2018).

The construction laws do not mention project timeline; there is no definition for the total time required for any project from planning to implementation. Notably, they also lack an emergency action plan that fits the Syrian Civil War ramifications. There is no comprehensive strategic plan that capable of fulfilling community's needs, goals, and aspirations, as pointed out by another expert professional interviewee while discussing the redevelopment projects especially Marota city project. According to him, "no compensation, no housing alternatives and absolutely, no community engagement in the decision-making process." This is clearly remarkable in Decree No. 66 of 2012, which allowed Syrian authorities to redevelop areas of unauthorized housing and informal settlements with no warning of the demolitions and without offering any compensations. As per this law, they plan to demolish several residential neighborhoods such as Kafr Sousa, Basatin al-Razi, Mezzeh in the southwestern part of the Syrian capital, to be replaced by skyscrapers, hotels, and restaurants (Tahrir, 2019).

Rebuilding amidst and post-conflict is an extraordinary situation. Consequently, it is unreasonable to adopt construction laws of the typical general nature used in common conditions but building regulations capable of dealing with the emergencies' consequences where there is an urgent need to provide settlements for a mass population within a short time.

Therefore, the laws must be completely renewed by looking at the problems of construction in emergencies. Reconstruction cannot be carried out with laws designed for regular construction in peacetime because the emergency situation is completely different. The displaced resettlement in post-emergencies requires providing a huge number of accommodations within small spaces and restricted time by doing it in the best possible way and with the most fitting urban functionality and also with the presence of well-formed public spaces because people must love the place where they will live, they cannot be provided with a place that resembles a provisional settlement. Kleinschmidt (2015) declared that the average lodging in refugee camps had been increased from nine years to around seventeen years. In that matter, the Palestine refugee camps in Jordan prove that refugee camps remain in cities for more than three generations. They were instituted as temporal lodging with provisional construction materials but are not temporary anymore. As can be observed, the life span of these camps ranges from 50 to 60 years. Such lifespan gives a great indication that temporal camps are the cities of tomorrow. A closer look at the current situation of Jordan shows how Palestinian refugees camps strongly affected the Urban fabric of Jordan. While those camps were constructed as temporary lodging, the camp residents hit their roots in the land and settled and started sprawl in troublesome slums. Syrian refugees forced to flee their country and settle in camps at the northern borders, serious steps must be taken to solve the refugee camps problem to prevent any replication to what happened with Palestinian refugee camps. Short-lived solutions to refugees' camps' problems will not work anymore. Everyone pretends Zaatari will dissolve when the Syrian civil war ends (Smith, 2014), but the fact is that the camp, as of autumn 2021, has around 80,000 refugees who need an actual city that maintains their dignity, identity, and wellness. Kleichmidth (2015) argues that creating a city for the refugees aims to empower them to return as responsible people in dignity and reduce the dependence syndrome. Otherwise, social security issues and inequity problems arise; precisely, issues of gentrification, class division of society, and hatred when the poorer class meets the richer class. In this way, these temporary accommodations turn into informal cities. Consequently, there is an urgent need for a plan of action that reviews and revises the existing construction and reconstruction laws in Syria on informal housing, to develop city planning systems that suit the current phase. There is a need for high-level collaborations between the housing sector of the governorates, the local administrations, the Ministry of Housing, the Housing Council in the Housing Assembly, and the Housing Committees in the government.

In the Zaatari refugee camp's case, this sphere dealt with design regulations of the camp's settlements which are built based on standards rather than laws and regulations. As argued previously, the response of spatial planners and urban politicians to the refugees' urgent need for housing suddenly and in short time led them to employ incremental planning strategies to design the refugee camp based on numbers and minimum standards. At the international level, it is often the case that the design of refugee camps depends on manuals and guidelines that have been developed by humanitarian organizations such as UNHCR. Examples of those guidelines are the Handbook for Emergencies (UNHCR, 2007), Refugee Camp Planning and Construction Handbook (2000), and The Sphere Handbook: Humanitarian Charter and Minimum Standards in Disaster Response (2004) (Alshoubaki & Zazzara, 2020). Although Jordan has always been a hosting country for refugees, it has around 15 refugee camps ranging from 6 years old up to 70 years. Still, the current situation of refugee camps in Jordan reveals that the construction laws and town planning regulations lack appropriate strategies to construct refugee camps sustainably.

It appears that the "one size fits all" is the main approach for dealing with housing in emergencies; their working strategies are not outlined based on the crisis's context but rather they came to the emergency field, wherever it was and whenever the emergency happens, with a package of organizational, operational, and executive policies. Accordingly, the inflexibility of the technical standards, the response strategy, and temporary mindset in methodological approach shapes a very hazardous temporary character of these provisional settlements, creates serious urban problems, transforms these temporary settlements into slum-like neighborhoods, deforms the urban identity of the cities where they appear, creates isolated zones with no relationship with the city urban fabric. Consequently, building resilient camp settlement requires a project that looks to the future, in other words, a project with permanent characters,

4.3 Construction Laws and the Technical Standards Sphere

a context-specified approach that respects the refugees' needs and respects the urban identity.

The discussion of the two cases within the three spheres, illustrated in Fig. 5.2, could be summarized as the following: the spatial sphere on Damascus cases reveals the complexity of the spatial reality and the urban development in the post-conflict Damascus, primarily because of the incapacity of the current master plan to deal with damage degree. Organizing the informal zones that are already out of Damascus's organizational plan and dealing with the damage on the peripheral zones are the main issues needed to be solved in any plan to reconstruct Damascus. On another side, the spatial reality in the case of the Zaatari refugee camp showed how a provisional plan drawn based on standards transformed into a semi-structural city within around eight years. The diagnostic and assessment sphere on Damascus showed several economic, financial, legal, social, institutional, and governmental challenges that impact the reconstruction in post-war Damascus besides the absence of disasters management strategies, the opposed sanctions, and the chaotic actions from different actors. While in Zaatari, the analysis showed that the camp within a short time turned into a permanent anarchic urban zone with marginal living conditions.

The construction laws and technical standards sphere revealed that Damascus lacks a comprehensive national strategy capable of dealing with the ramification of the Syrian Civil War. Thus, no emergency action plan is connected to a specific time frame. At the same time, Zaatari lacks a context-specified approach; in fact, it is a plan based on numbers minimum standards. The rigid temporary housing techniques form zones of informalities that is at odds with the existing urban fabric (Fig. 4.2).

As the case studies of Damascus and the Zaatari camp exemplify, the absence of a wide-ranging theory in spatial planning that covers post-conflict situation for

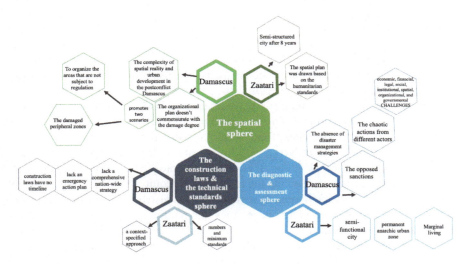

Fig. 4.2 The discussion spheres. Ref: The author 2021

providing temporary living environment necessitates having a conceptual framework that can be referred to as Urban Emergency Integrated Planning [UEIP].

4.4 UEIP: Urban Emergency Integrated Planning

The resettlement of refugees and returnees in post-conflict and post-war situations is a very extended, complex, and intertwined issue that affected by different dimensions, that are the political dimension, the historical dimension, the social dimension, the time dimension, and the economic dimension, which are crucial factors that impact the resettlement process in post-conflict situations. Consequently, the availability of political stability and national security is a fundamental step before starting any reconstruction plans as it is impossible to plan for reconstruction within an unknown horizon full of violence and terrorism. The lack of peace slows down the reconstruction process in Syria due to the restrictions imposed by local civil ministers or the global sanctions imposed on the Syrian regime by the US and EU. However, according to the German Institute for International and Security Affairs "SWP" (2020), reconstruction in Syria is being done by different actors who implemented projects at the local level. Still, obviously, up to now, there is no comprehensive nationwide program for managing the reconstruction in Syria. Secondly, the social dimension has a vital role in leading the resettlement process during reconstruction. Generally, the reconstruction discussions revolve around the buildings and stone conservations and neglect that reconstruction means urban regeneration by reclaiming the city's urban identity, in other words, cities that resemble the culture, the history, and the identity of the Syrian community. For this reason, the cultural and social dimension requires the active participation of the local society. Another critical point that links the social dimension with the historical dimension is the entry of giant global foreign companies in the reconstruction, threatening Damascus's history and identity. Therefore, there must be serious initiatives that encourage local housing cooperative associations that draw reconstructed reconstruction plans with the local community and western experiences.

Thirdly, the economic dimension plays an essential role in managing the resettlement process. Since if there is no fund, that means no reconstruction and even no materials for the reconstruction. The lack of reconstruction funds made very timid reconstruction operations in Syria, up to now, and took place through individual acts to restore parts of their homes that include simple structural reconstruction to have a shelter. Fourthly, organizing the resettlement requires time, starting from the evaluation to the implementation. In parallel, time is also a highly critical factor in framing an action plan for urgent necessities that require quick responses, to solve the paradox between the urgent need for a residential city that covers the needs of large numbers of residents within a tight and limited time, by ensuring high-quality reconstruction projects but within a short-time frame.

To address the above, it appears that the current integrated urban planning theory needs to be adjusted and further integrated to be usable in post-emergency situations.

4.4 UEIP: Urban Emergency Integrated Planning

The Urban Emergency Integrated Plan (UEIP) corresponds to the planning approach's heterogeneous nature within the emergency context, especially conflicts and wars. First, it can expand its horizontal integration in spatial planning to a specific timeframe that integrates social, health care, economic, security, and environmental aspects. Second, it can expand its vertical integration by including more levels of governance and engaging the local community, humanitarian organizations, refugees, and returnees in the decision-making process, the agenda preparation, and the project implementation.

The UEIP conceptual framework links the refined, integrated planning approach with the cycle of emergency management and planning, highlighting the time as a critical factor within two dimensions: the implementation time and the very urgent, prompt need for a housing solution within a short period. That assists the stricken cities to move from the state of emergency to the state of resilience by employing permanent, sustainable solutions, in which the new ad hoc urban politics for post-conflict resettlement can address the need for a definitive city for both refugees and returnees and will relinquish the temporary refugee camps as abrupt normative solutions.

The framework potentially helps to create a set of planning actions aimed at facing and solving real problems through design strategies that stemmed from the uncertainty of controlling future events. This can be done through defining the levels and typologies of integrated spatial planning capable of building sustainable resettlement in urban emergencies and regulating the expropriation for public utilities. There should be the ability to introduce rules for the rehabilitation and expansion of cities, giving close attention to the precarious conditions and hygiene in many urban areas and mainly linking to the rapid population growth and rapid urban growth to improve the cities' performance and capacity. While driven from the case studies in this research, the UEIP potentially indicates the route for constructing and restructuring the existing cities in similar situations to rise again, starting from the evaluation process until the implementation. The following steps detailed below led to the development of this framework.

First Step: Identifying specific codes related to planning in emergencies. The first cycle codes regarding integrated planning were developed from a systematic and critical review of the literature as discussed previously in Chap. 2, and they are strategic, sustainable, comprehensive, participative, operational, financial resources.

The second cycle codes were developed from the semi-structured interviews with refugees (male and females) in Zaatari refugee camp, experts in organizing the camp from the UNHCR, and experts in the reconstruction field in Damascus, Syria, academics and researchers in urban planning, environmental engineering, habitat engineering, and structural engineering. The codes included hierarchal scaling, economic, social, financial, spatial, institutional, organizational, diagnostical, space-time.

The first and second cycle codes are illustrated in Fig. 4.3.

Second Step: Reviewing the current emergency management cycle, which governs the management of natural incidences and human-made disasters.

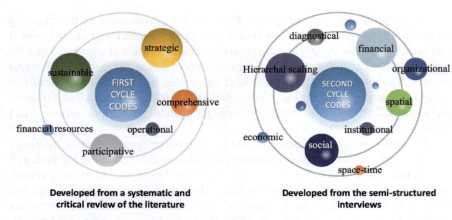

Fig. 4.3 The developed codes for building the new theoretical framework. Ref: The author, 2021

The analysis of case studies showed that the existing emergency management cycle does not correspond with the scale of the war damage because of the following reasons: The emergency cycle's major phases, namely, prevention, preparedness, mitigation, response, and recovery are more appropriate in dealing with natural incidents, but the post-war situation is to some extent different. While there might be some similarities, there are inherent differences. For example, war, as a catastrophe, cannot be prevented in the same way of preventing disaster risks, and therefore, it is impossible to outline excessive permanent protection measures. The first required response to human-made catastrophes, in particular, wars and conflicts, to deal with the urban emergency is a diagnostic evaluation capable of evaluating the context and determining the needs to assess the situation spatially and organizationally. The second post-war emergency management phase should be about the regulating phase, in which reconstruction laws and legislations should be enacted. The legislated laws should look to emergency with a vision on permanent solutions because what regulates a building's design in peacetime might not fit and not applicable to post-war reconstruction. The third phase should be the strategic planning phase, which happens directly after the laws' legislation, which determines a sustainable orientation toward the implementation by engaging local actors keeping strong coordination between cities, governorates, and municipalities through mayors by forming operation, planning, and technical groups which commingle refugees (Syrians in this research) and other experts from other realties who have the habit of thinking in urban and spatial planning also in emergencies. In this phase, it is essential to organize the arrangement of actions in a specific timeframe putting together all the challenges, threats, and opportunities of the reconstruction. The final phase is the reconstruction's operationalization, which puts the methodological decision in practice. It should guarantee an active engagement of the displaced community in the reconstruction process to maintain the city's urban identity and invest in all available resources. The above are shown in Fig. 4.4.

4.4 UEIP: Urban Emergency Integrated Planning

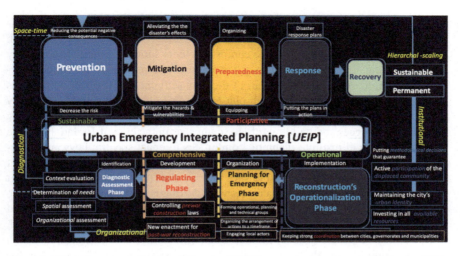

Fig. 4.4 Urban Emergency Integrated Planning [UEIP] conceptual framework. The author 2020

Through undertaking the necessary steps described, the UEIP controls the direct urbicide and indirect urbicide phenomena. It encompasses the organization of the construction process within the four main phases in a time–space frame to attain the best planning solution within an appropriate time. The UEIP in the direct urbicide will regulate a quick reconstruction process linked to the city's history and identity. For this reason, it starts with evaluating the current damage through spatial assessment and determining the war victim's needs through need and organizational evaluation; in this phase, the assessments should be done within 30–45 days since the displaced population return which is according to the experts in reconstruction the average time required to assess and analyze the local needs.

In fact, in the case of post-war scenarios, it is impossible to predict if the city will go through war or conflict. Consequently, cities often don't have planning regulations or strategies to deal with the ramifications of the war. Therefore, this phase requires more time to control the pre-war laws and to enact new ones capable of dealing with the size of the damage. Then in the planning phase, it is essential to organize the arrangement of actions within a specific time frame maintaining active participation of the displaced population. It should not exceed 60–80 days which is the average time recommended by experts in reconstruction to plan the reconstruction and to organize the action plan then to move for the last phase, the reconstruction's operationalization phase. The implementation of all plans should be with strong coordination between cities, governorates, and municipalities.

In parallel, implementing the UEIP in the indirect urbicide scenarios will reduce the negative consequences of the quick temporary solutions used in designing refugee camps, as seen in the Zaatari camp. The diagnostic phases in this situation should be completed within 30–120 days of the refugee's arrival to the hosting country which is the time according to the refugees they can cope with the provisional life conditions. Evaluating the site context and assessing the refugee needs to be prepared with the minimum time. In this phase, no camps and tents should be built. The strategy should be using alternative housing such as vacant buildings and other public structures while preparing the spatial plan of the new settlements. The second phase is the regulating phase divided into sub-phases: the first sub-phase should be already outlined before any displacement, especially in countries that have a profound history in receiving refugees and building refugee camps, as in the case of Jordan. Here, the government should institute planning committees to enact specific laws and determine probable locations in the country's master plan capable of being new-settlement to receive refugees. This is helpful to save time for the site selection and the context evaluation. The second sub-phase crosses with the diagnostic phase and continues to develop the appropriate regulations that are stemmed from the refugee's needs and aspirations. The third phase organizes the emergency phase by forming technical, operational, and planning groups that work together with the refugees in which the time required shouldn't exceed 30–60 days to start the last phase that is the reconstruction's operationalization.

4.5 Conclusion

Spatial planning in a post-conflict situation is a complex issue. It requires ad hoc strategies that deal with the emergency and the conflict ramifications using a sustainable approach to create a resilient built environment with permanent solutions. Integrated planning provides an adaptable mechanism, and it is socially responsible for enhancing the citizens' life quality with optimum living conditions for current and upcoming generations. This mechanism seeks to provide sustainable and resilient planning solutions in addition to the involvement of various stakeholders and local communities in the planning and management processes. The absence of the time factor in the integrated planning theory makes this approach lack the credibility to be adapted alone in emergency planning and to create permanent housing solutions for war victims. This has made it necessary to develop a new comprehensive conceptual framework (i.e., the UEIP) for planning in an emergency involving the post-conflict resettlement process.

References

Al-Jablawi. (2018). Rebuilding amidst conflict: Law 10 and its implications. Atlantic Council. Retrieved from https://www.atlanticcouncil.org/blogs/syriasource/rebuilding-amidst-conflict-law-10-and-its-implications/.

Alshoubaki, H., & Zazzara, L. (2020). The fragility in the land of refugees: Jordan and irrepressible phenomenon of refugee camps. *Journal of International Studies, 13*(1), 123–142. https://doi.org/10.14254/2071-8330.2020/13-1/8

References

Blatter, J. K., Janning, F., & Wagemann, C. (2007). Qualitative Politikanalyse: Eine Einführung in Forschungsansätze und Methoden. Wiesbaden: VS Verlag für Sozialwissenschaften | GWV Fachverlage GmbH Wiesbaden.

Clerc, V. (2014). Informal settlements in the Syrian conflict: Urban planning as a weapon. *Built Environment, 40*(1), 34–51.

Fuccaro, N. (2003). Ethnicity and the city: The Kurdish quarter of Damascus between ottoman and French rule, c. 1724–1946. *Urban History, 30*(2), 206–224.

Hamedi, S. (2018). Minister of housing to Al-Watan: Amending the expropriation law is not proposed and Laws 66, 10 and 23 solve housing problems. Retrieved May, 2020, from https://alwatan.sy/archives/150723

Kleinschmidt, K. (2015). Interview by Conner Maher. January. Zaatari Refugee Camp, Jordan.

Lazareva, I. (2016, June 08). 'We came for 15 days... but three years on we STILL live here': Inside Jordan's sprawling Zaatari refugee camp - home to 80,000 migrants fleeing war in Syria. from http://www.dailymail.co.uk/news.

Leach, J., Mulhall, R., Rogers, C., & Bryson, J. (2019). Reading cities: Developing an urban diagnostics approach for identifying integrated urban problems with application to the city of Birmingham, UK. Retrieved from https://www.sciencedirect.com/science/article/pii/S0264275118303093.

Ledwith, A., & Smith, D. (2014). Zaatari: The Instant City (Rep.). An Affordable Housing Institute Publication. Retrieved from http://sigus.scripts.mit.edu/x/files/Zaatari/AHIPublication.pdf.

Naito, M. (1988). From the walled inner city to the urban periphery: Changing phases of residential separation in Damascus (Vol. 102). Geographical Studies & Japan.

OHCHR. (2018). General Assembly—ohchr.org. Retrieved from https://www.ohchr.org/Documents/HRBodies/HRCouncil/CoISyria/A-HRC-37-72_EN.pdf.

Radford, T. (2016). *Refugee camps are the "cities of tomorrow", says aid expert*. Dezeen. Retrieved from https://www.dezeen.com/2015/11/23/refugee-camps-cities-of-tomorrow-killian-kleinschmidt-interview-humanitarian-aid-expert/.

Rodgers, L., Trowsdale, A., & Bryson, M. (2018, March 29). Eastern ghouta Syria: The neighbourhoods below the bombs. BBC News. Retrieved from https://www.bbc.com/news/world-middle-east-43154146.

SWP. (2020). SWP research paper—swp-berlin.org. Retrieved from https://www.swp-berlin.org/publications/products/research_papers/2020RP11_ReconstructionSyria.

Tahrir. (2019). TIMEP brief: Law no. 10 of 2018: Housing, land, and property. TIMEP. Retrieved from https://timep.org/reports-briefings/timep-brief-law-no-10-of-2018-housing-land-and-property/.

UNHCR. (2007), Handbook for Emergencies, Genève: United nations high commissioner for refugees.

UNHCR. (2014). Global strategy for settlement and shelter, A UNHCR Strategy 2014–2018 (1211 edn., Vol. 2). United Nations High Commissioner for Refugees.

UNHCR. (2021). Jordan: Zaatari Refugee Camp fact sheet. Retrieved from https://reliefweb.int/sites/reliefweb.int/files/resources/06%20Zaatari%20Fact%20Sheet%20June%202021.pdf

UNITAR-UNOSAT. (2013). Evolution of Al Zaatari refugee camp, Mafraq Governorate, Jordan (as of 14 May 2013)—jordan. ReliefWeb. Retrieved from https://reliefweb.int/map/jordan/evolution-al-zaatari-refugee-camp-mafraq-governorate-jordan-14-may-2013.

United Nations High Commissioner for Refugees. (2015a, June 18). Worldwide displacement hits all-time high as war and persecution increase. Retrieved November 08, 2016, from http://www.unhcr.org/news/latest/2015a/6/558193896/worldwide-displacement-hits-all-time-high-war-persecution-increase.html

United Nations High Commissioner for Refugees. (2015b). UNHCR Global Trends 2015b. Retrieved from http://www.unhcr.org/statistics/unhcrstats/576408cd7/unhcr-global-trends-2015b.html.

Wissenschaft, S. (2020). *SWP research paper—swp-berlin.org*. Retrieved from https://www.swpberlin.org/publications/products/research_papers/2020RP11_ReconstructionSyria.pdf.

Chapter 5
Concluding Discussions

Abstract When cities pass under extraordinary events that require exceptional tools to manage their transformation, this chapter discusses the importance of this study to urban planning and future research. It argues the temporary city hypothesis policy presented by this study. The UEIP framework was built to respond to emergencies and organize the post-conflict issue reconstruction since the temporary re-settlements play a crucial role in emergency scenarios to reinforce the recovery and accomplish the reconstruction process.

Keywords UEIP · Temporary city

5.1 UEIP and FUTURE Directions

The future of post-war urban emergency response including reconstruction requires implementing strategies to maintain the war victims' right to a city, not a shelter nor a camp. Refugees and displaced people need a real, functional, and permanent city project. As appears, the integrated planning theory, urban emergency management, and post-conflict reconstruction strategies alone are incapable to address the need for designing fully-functional cities in short periods, for two types of war victims, namely, refugees in a hosting country and returnees to their homeland. The UEIP conceptual framework in fact links urbicide, urban emergency management, and the integrated planning theory to create long-term strategies that are capable of providing permanent outcomes. The construction of this framework contributes to the discourse on what is called "the temporary city hypothesis" to synthesize the phenomenon and draw the best practice in spatial planning capable of organizing the issue under investigation.

The temporary city hypothesis **is** about a spatial organization that deals with the sudden population influx in displacement and post-war reconstruction cases. The temporary city concept is connected with time as a crucial factor in providing housing for those in need through employing *Temporization* as a technical approach for any urban space in an emergency by using integrated planning techniques to construct provisional restorations that are urgently needed in short or medium time, which is essential to develop a more permanent revival. To benefit from the temporality idea in sense of saving time to provide reconstruction and habitat to people within limited time, the temporary urbanism will create typologies to design settlements and will use temporary techniques in restoration and rehabilitation. The Population in Syria is now divided into two strata. The first one covers the refugees' stratum who lives in camps in poor conditions as seen in the case of Zaatari refugee camp. The second stratum includes the urban refugees, and the internally displaced persons who fled internally from the zones under attack into safer areas within the same country as discussed in Damascus city's case.

From one side the Syrian returnees from refugee camps wouldn't wish to be in conditions of refuge again in their own country after return. They will not accept similar solutions or the same housing conditions and techniques that used in camp design as mentioned by a Syrian refugee interviewee "When we return, we want to return in our homes with dignity, we will not accept to be refugees in our homeland." Also, those refugees who were asylum seekers in the European countries will not accept to live in temporary settlements but rather they are willing for a new modern planning with public spaces, sufficient public transportation that link the whole Syrian governorate together, especially the governorate centers.

The post-conflict reconstruction works are the first signs of the peacebuilding process and an essential step in healing the wounded cities (UNHCR, 1996). However, the reconstruction works are often long-lasting within a chaotic atmosphere, aiming at regaining the normalcy of life after the man-made catastrophes. The temporary re-settlements play a key role in emergency scenarios to reinforce the recovery and to accomplish the reconstruction process (European Civil Protection and Humanitarian Aid Operations, 2017). Wars turn our cities topsy-turvy where houses are totally or partially destroyed, the infrastructure is missing, high polluted environments, dirtiness and lack of hygiene, accordingly to move from the state of emergency to the state of resilience, we have to pass through the temporary resettlement in order to decrease the human losses resulting from the lack of a healthy environment and to resume the normal functionality of life as illustrated in Fig. 5.1.

The transitional period between the emergency event and the reconstruction works is very critical because we are not moving directly from rescue/return to rebuild, from emergency shelter to durable house, from critical repairs to infrastructure or from relief to resilience. But there is a transitional period in which the stricken communities need a full functional city with appropriate infrastructure.

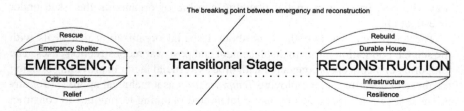

Fig. 5.1 The resettlement issue from emergency to reconstruction. The author 2020

5.1 UEIP and FUTURE Directions

The aim of this research was to tie-up the temporary city within the emergency cycle's major phases: prevention, preparedness, mitigation, response, and recovery. Case studies showed that temporary cities are not in fact that much "temporary," highlighting the need for a city that matches the local reality rather than an emergency shelter, and to devote the attention toward the significant role of public spaces in temporary accommodation as healing zones from the disasters through maintaining the social relations and as places of emergency qualified with appropriate infrastructure ready to accommodate any new displacement. This means studying the entire city as a whole project, not as fragmented parts. For this reason, the temporary city hypothesis is about a project that is able to provide a better-quality settlement than what was there before the conflict.

In emergencies, especially in post-conflict situations, the spatial planning laws of a general nature in normal situations are not enough, but here we need projects; we need laws that allow the possibility of creating projects that correspond with the scale of damage left by the war. We have to build cities not as they were before, but we have to sustainably build cities that function better, considering the future in mind. To work better means not only more beauty but more comfort. Working better also means lower costs, that is, to construct the best urban settlements with the lowest cost, to keep all urbanization well. The best practice means that investment in reconstruction is made in the right way. Therefore, the laws must be completely renewed by looking at the post-war and post-conflict issues. Reconstruction cannot be carried out with laws that have been designed to regulate construction in times of peace because the emergency is a completely another scenario, with its time and budget restrictions and the involvement of numerous external stakeholders. The emergency scenario requires providing the greatest possible number of houses within small areas in the best possible way within the shortest time and with high urban functionality and beauty of public spaces because people must attach to the place where they will live for unknown months or years. They cannot be sent to a place that resembles a temporary settlement. In the Damascus case, these new parts should have been connected to the pre-war Damascus as the spatial analysis of the city demonstrated. Damascus is a city with multi historical layers which must be respected by any reconstruction project. They must be well-coordinated with Damascus's urban form but must also be a growth that allows giving an identity to the new parts. On the one hand, they must be well-connected with other cities in new parts, while on the other hand, the new parts must not feel peripheral but must have a new neighborhood identity. This is a critical point because it creates a united city. As discussed, the majority of the demographic of Damascus are the Muslim population. Therefore, to design a city that will be lived in by a Muslim is not so simple because Muslim culture tends to maintain high privacy in design, apparently in this context, the culture matters now. This however, can be slightly different in different Muslim countries, as for example in Syria, this issue appears less than in other Arab countries.

From another perspective, the analysis of the Zaatari refugee camp led to realize that a temporary settlement, in reality, is not temporary because they implement permanent. It must be understood that when a refugee camp was built, the camp, certainly, has some identity aspects. Therefore, these aspects must be known and included in the renovation projects, which are implemented in the camp. They can be streets; they can be the district's orientation, they can be small squares formed by refugees themselves, small places that have been used for supermarkets, or streets that have become market streets. In sum, there are these elements of a city in the camp, as we saw and discussed previously in the Zaatari camp case.

As an innovative conceptual framework, UEIP sets multiple direction toward a new urban planning system that has to cope with the emergency from its start. It is not an ordinary management of urban transformation but extraordinary management of the reconstruction of the entire part of the cities that have been destroyed or, damaged. Here additional tools are needed to respect the rights of the displaced people who will return to their home land. Hence, the need to create conditions that favor the return of the population. So, of course, we need an approach that considers the housing of the displaced population while the parts of the cities are under the rebuilt because this population needs to remain attached to those parts under reconstruction. When they return, they should also be able to work on the reconstruction projects while constituting itself so that the population binds themselves back to this new habitat, otherwise, they will always be a strange population. This also means that the new parts of the city that need to be re-created should not be left to the free market, that is to the operation of poor construction speculation. A reconstruction project that is by a company that may come up from abroad takes the land and builds and then sells the houses freely because that means that you destroy the social fabric.

In this matter, an urgent need for reconstruction programs that control how the companies must build the new parts, how they can step in, and how the houses that are produced and other projects can go on the market. In sum, it must be a strongly controlled process by the locals because it is the only way to guarantee a social policy. Because the foreign companies alone will not give proper attention to the Syrian society, but they are interested in selling at the best possible price as quickly as possible for what they had built. Then, among other critical things, there is a need for strong public control because the quality of the pre-war projects should be improved and replaced with a better one. This is along with "building back better." Therefore, high-quality projects cannot be attained if the construction is entrusted without a strong program that controls all the aspects of the context. The reconstruction needs to be linked to a very detailed program that controls how the population is allowed to participate during construction and a program that also controls the quality of the urban organization that is being rebuilt. It means the relationship with the existing city, together with this new zone, can improve this organization. The relationship concerns public services; the relationship is the viability; the quality with the environment also because the infrastructure, aqueducts, purifiers, and the main services must function normally. All this cannot be torn apart but must be controlled in a general spatial design, probably, in such a situation, as it is difficult to establish, which is the succession of interventions. In other words, what comes first and what comes later because now the idea is still quite approximate; probably, the organization should begin from a general hierarchal master plan, city by city that includes all the areas that need to be built and also those that need to be rebuilt again. The newly planned areas in this master plan must establish the criteria first of all to make an urban fabric

5.1 UEIP and FUTURE Directions

that is always continuous, coherent, cohesive, well connected; it is not a fabric in pieces. Then to establish some criteria for the urban quality of what is being proposed. That is, to say, how urbanization will be done, how houses will be built, and with what quality, what kind of people should go to live there. This means it is not a free market, but it is established that a certain area must be accessible to popular consumption to avoid the ghost cities' phenomenon. In sum, the houses must meet these criteria. Then, part by part within this master plan and constructive programs that respond to general coordination criteria and at the same time will have to respond to projects that have their own autonomy within this sector. So, the master plan is very important, and then after the master plan, we need very detailed projects of the type of urbanization that are going to be done. The master plan must consider all the aspects of the built environment and it should also organize the transport system, the distribution of the schools, the distribution of the health system, security and so on. Therefore, all planning aspects must be consistent with a global framework given in the master plan and then be developed through area projects. This post-war environment should be defined by a law dedicated to reconstruction, so we need a law that establishes which is the ordinary structure of the planning process, that is, what is there when there is no war and no reconstruction, but it also takes a specific program for reconstruction that defines the extraordinary instruments. These extraordinary instruments must have the purpose of serving as best as possible the population who have been affected.

Consequently, there is a need for a fairly integrated urban planning basis but with clear objectives at the moment in Syria. The premise of these objectives must be, on the one hand, the maximum public benefit and the public interest of all. On the other hand, the maximum possible advancement of modernization can be obtained from the parts that are being rebuilt because one cannot start from urbanization that was already old and malfunctioned even before the war. However, it must start with a new system that works better and guarantees that it will sustainably function in the future. So, it takes a considerable effort, but there is no such effort in Syria because they don't have the slightest preparation for this kind of emergency program of their own. So, in the first phase and under the coordination of the Syrian republic and under strong coordination between the cities, the municipalities, and the mayors, it would take operation groups, planning groups, and technical groups, which should be mixed of Syrians and people from a reality that has the habit of thinking about planning, and emergencies because it is not the political and economic planning of ex-communist countries but something different. Urban planning is a system of thought that serves to build the modern city but with close attention to the community's history and culture, the need of the Arab and Islamic culture which is favorable by the Syrians themselves but on the other hand it has the technical ability to think in a contemporary city planning and to do this we need not only the designers, architects, engineers, but it also requires the city planners.

5.2 Conclusion

Conflict-affected cities represent the biggest and the most complicated threat to human life, and one of the most interlaced urban phenomena. Syria is considered one of the most brutal urban conflicts in recent years, killing and making homeless hundreds of thousands of people, torn the nation apart, and set back the standard of living by decades (The International Institute for Strategic Studies [IISS], 2017). About 5.6 million Syrians are refugees around the globe, while another 6.2 million people are displaced within Syria. Nearly 12 million people in Syria need humanitarian assistance (World Vision, 2020).

This book examined the adoption of the integrated approach in planning during the emergency, to plan adequate cities for the war victims who lost their houses. The discussion focused on the war victims and their right to a city within two perspectives: First, as refugees where they need urgent housing in the hosting countries but more than a refugee camp. Second, for the returnees to their home countries who find nothing rather than rubbles and partial remains of their cities.

The two cases: the Damascus city in Syria and the Zaatari camp in Jordan reflect the same complexity issue in the urgent need for housing, but a real, permanent one with appropriate services that ensure them with convenient living conditions by developing a new urban agenda which is capable of dealing with the housing demands after the conflict in means of a need for a real city not only a temporary shelter, of sharpening a distinctive approach in integrated planning in terms of logistical executive, administrative, and legislative planning which is able to deal with the current urban challenges of post-conflict environments in accordance with different political and humanitarian institutions. The remedy to this challenge can go through a fundamental refinement of the ongoing integrated planning process with a particular link to the revised cycle of urban emergency management.

The study proposes a new theoretical framework toward planning in emergency "Urban Emergency Integrated planning" [UEIP]. The "UEIP" corresponds to the heterogeneous nature of the planning approach within the situation of emergency—especially conflicts and wars. This framework, primarily justified the current integrated urban planning theory. It was firstly done by broadening its horizontal integration in spatial planning to a specific timeframe that integrates social, health care, economic, security, and environmental aspects. Secondly, it expanded the vertical integration of the theory by including more levels of governance systems, such as engaging the local community, the humanitarian organizations, refugees, and returnees in the decision-making process, the agenda preparation, and the project implementation. Then, the refined, integrated planning approach was connected the cycle of emergency management and planning focusing on time as a critical factor within two dimensions: the implementation time and the very urgent, prompt need for a housing solution within a short period.

The city in the camp and the camp in the city

The temporary vs. the permanent

The shelter vs. the home

The displacement vs. the right to a city

All these concepts send clear signals to take serious steps in spatial planning during emergencies. Planning in emergencies, whether for refugees or the returnees, needs an integrated urban policy that sustainably provides well-designed spaces, which are capable of ensuring a better life quality and improved urban environments in the long run

References

European Civil Protection and Humanitarian Aid Operations. (2017). Shelter and settlement guidelines—European commission. Retrieved from https://ec.europa.eu/echo/files/policies/sectoral/shelter_and_settlement_guidelines.pdf.

UNHCR. (1996). Healing the wounds: Refugees, reconstruction and reconciliation, report of the Second Conference at Princeton University 30 June—1 July 1996, sponsored jointly by United Nations high commissioner for refugees and international peace academy. Refworld. Retrived from https://www.refworld.org/docid/3ae68f3e0.html.

World Vision. (2020). Fears and Dreams of Syrian children. Retrieved from https://www.wvi.org/fearsanddreamscontinued/

Index

A
Ada Louise Huxtable, 50
Al-Hussin camp, 21
Amman, 3, 8, 15, 17, 18, 20, 21, 24, 34, 35, 63, 85, 86

B
Baqa'a camp, 8, 9

C
Camp, 1–6, 8–10, 12, 13, 15–21, 24, 25, 27, 30, 33–35, 37, 38, 44, 50, 51, 63, 75, 85, 88–91, 93, 97–100, 102–107, 109, 111, 115–117, 120, 121
Civil war, 1, 2, 5, 6, 18, 44–48, 76, 82, 85, 88, 90, 97, 104, 106
Conflicts, 1, 5, 6, 27, 47, 50, 57, 58, 109, 110, 120
Construction, 2, 5, 6, 10, 13, 25, 28, 38, 43, 48, 50, 57, 63, 64, 68, 69, 75, 80, 84, 86, 93, 97–99, 103–107, 111, 115, 117, 118
Construction Laws, 104

D
Damascus, 1–5, 26, 27, 38, 63–81, 83, 85, 93, 97–101, 104, 107–109, 116, 117, 120
Decree 66, 81, 83
Diagnostic sphere, 100
Displaced, 1, 5, 6, 11, 12, 15, 26–28, 33, 37, 45, 53, 63, 76, 79, 80, 85, 97, 105, 110, 111, 115, 116, 118, 120

E
Emergency, 2, 5, 7, 8, 10, 12, 13, 25, 27, 29, 31, 33–35, 37, 38, 43, 48, 51, 53–55, 59, 63, 90, 98, 100, 103, 105–110, 112, 115–121

F
Federal Emergency Management Agency (FEMA), 55

H
Housing, 1, 2, 5, 13, 27, 28, 30, 31, 33, 37, 44–46, 53, 56, 57, 63, 73, 76, 78, 80–85, 88, 90, 93, 97–102, 104–109, 112, 115, 116, 118, 120

I
Indirect urbicide, 5, 37, 38, 43, 44, 48, 50, 63, 93, 100, 111
Informal settlements, 63, 64, 74, 75, 83, 98, 105
Integrated planning, 43, 56–58, 109, 112, 115, 120
Internally Displaced Person (IDP), 78
Italy, 27, 28

J
Jordan, 1, 2, 3, 6, 8, 12, 17–21, 26, 27, 33–35, 38, 50, 53, 63, 85, 86, 88, 89, 93, 97, 98, 105, 106, 112, 120
Amman, 15

L
L'Aquila, 27–29
Law 10, 63, 64, 81, 82, 104
Law 9, 63, 81, 84
Law No. 33, 83

M
Marota City, 81, 82
Marshal Berman, 50

P
Palestine, 8, 20, 21, 26, 85, 105
Palestinian, 6, 8, 15, 17, 20, 21, 27, 34, 45, 50, 73, 74, 105
Permanent, 1, 2, 6, 8, 9, 16, 18, 20, 24, 25, 33, 34, 37, 43, 55, 58, 93, 100, 102, 106, 107, 109, 110, 112, 115, 117, 120, 121
Planning, 2, 5, 8, 10, 12, 13, 16, 25, 28, 34, 37, 38, 43, 44, 48, 50–52, 54–59, 63–65, 67, 68, 70, 72–74, 82–86, 88, 90, 91, 93, 97–99, 101–112, 115–121
  integrated planning, 56
  permanent, 43
  reconstruction, 51
  sustainable, 43
Post-conflict, 51, 53, 82
Postconflict Reconstruction (PCR), 5, 51–53

R
Reconstruction, 2, 5, 10, 25, 33, 38, 50–53, 64, 76, 80–82, 84, 85, 93, 97, 98, 101, 104, 106–112, 115–118
  temporization, 115
Refugee, 1–10, 12–21, 24–27, 30, 33–35, 37, 38, 43, 44, 48, 50, 51, 53, 55, 59, 63, 85, 88, 90–93, 97–100, 102–107, 109, 111, 116, 117, 120
Refugee camps, 5, 6, 8, 10, 34, 50, 100
  Al-Baqa'a camp, 8
  Zaatari refugee camp, 2

S
Settlement, 1, 5, 8, 10, 13, 15–17, 21, 24, 25, 28, 38, 48, 74, 88, 91, 100, 103–106, 112, 117
  Italian, 1

Shelters, 1, 6, 9, 10, 12, 27, 31, 33, 91, 92, 100, 103
  caravans, 10
  internally displaced persons, 1
Slum, 1, 16, 38, 50, 83, 88, 99, 106
Space, 9, 10, 13, 16, 17, 21, 25, 34, 43, 50, 55, 56, 58, 63, 64, 68, 90, 92, 98, 103, 104, 109, 111, 115
Spatial, 1, 2, 5, 6, 9, 10, 12, 13, 15, 16, 20, 34, 37, 38, 51, 55, 56, 58, 64, 82, 88, 90, 91, 93, 97–104, 106, 107, 109–112, 115, 117, 118, 120, 121
Spatial sphere, The, 98
Sustainability, 28, 55, 57
Sustainable, 2, 5, 28, 43, 51, 54–58, 97, 100, 102, 109, 110, 112
Syria
  Syrian refugees, 2–5, 18, 26, 27, 30, 38, 45–47, 53, 63, 64, 68, 72–74, 76, 80–82, 84, 85, 88, 89, 93, 98, 99, 101, 103–106, 108, 109, 116, 117, 119, 120
Syrian civil war, 1

T
Temporary, 1, 2, 5, 6, 8, 10, 13, 16, 18, 20, 21, 25, 27–29, 33–35, 37, 38, 43, 44, 48, 77, 78, 88, 90, 92, 93, 97, 99, 100, 103, 105–109, 111, 115–117, 120, 121
  shelters, 1
Temporary city, 1
The Urbicide, 43
Transformation, 1, 8–10, 13, 14, 16–18, 21, 25, 35, 38, 43, 51, 64, 65, 72, 88, 90, 93, 98–100, 102, 104, 115, 118
  conflicts, 1
  migration, 1
  natural incidents, 1

U
UN Development Program (UNDP), 56, 58
UN-Habitat, 52, 56
United Nations Institute for Training and Research (UNITAR), 47, 85
UN Operational Satellite Application Program (UNOSAT), 47
UN Refugee Agency (UNHCR), 2, 6–10, 12, 19–21, 27, 30, 33, 35, 45, 50, 53, 88–92, 100, 102, 104, 106, 109, 116
UN Relief and Works Agency for Palestine (UNRWA), 8, 21, 35

Index

Urban, 1, 2, 5–8, 10, 13, 15–18, 21, 24, 25, 27–30, 33–35, 37, 38, 43, 44, 47, 50, 51, 54–58, 63–68, 70, 72–76, 79, 81–86, 88, 90, 93, 97–102, 104–110, 115, 117–121
    housing, 90
    urban identity, 1
    urban scenario, 86
Urban destruction, 37, 43, 57
Urban development, 17, 51, 55, 56, 58, 63, 70, 87, 93, 98, 99, 107
    construction laws, 104
    diagnostic sphere, 100
    spatial sphere, 98
    technical standards sphere, 104
Urban Emergency Integrated Plan, 109
Urban Emergency Integrated Planning (UEIP), 2, 38, 97, 108, 109, 111, 112, 115, 118, 120
    UEIP, 109
Urban fabric, 1, 5, 7, 8, 13, 16, 17, 24, 25, 27, 28, 34, 35, 37, 44, 51, 73, 75, 76, 93, 98, 100, 106, 107, 118
Urbanism, 17, 34, 44, 64, 68, 70–72, 116
Urbanization, 1, 26, 56, 74, 86, 117, 119
    rapid urbanization, 1
Urban planners, 35, 44, 57
Urban Policy, 87
Urbicide, 5, 37, 38, 43–45, 48, 50, 51, 63, 93, 100, 111, 115
    direct urbicide, 43
    indirect urbicide, 43

W

War, 1
    War victims, 6, 7, 20, 26, 34, 45, 63, 68, 70, 74, 75, 79, 82, 98, 99, 101, 105, 107
war victims' right to a city, 115
World Health Organization (WHO), 45

Z

Zaatari, 2–5, 8, 9, 11, 18–21, 35, 38, 63, 85, 88–93, 97–100, 102–104, 106, 107, 109, 111, 116, 117, 120
Zaatari camp, 10, 18, 20, 63, 88, 90, 93, 100, 102, 118

Printed by Printforce, the Netherlands